MW00710100

GREAT MENU GRAPHICS

GREAT MENU GRAPHICS

by the Editors of PBC International

PBC International, Inc. • Glen Cove, New York

Copyright © 1989 by PBC International, Inc.
All rights reserved. No part of this book may be reproduced in any form whatsoever without written permission of the publisher. For information about this book write: PBC International, One School Street, Glen Cove, NY 11542.

Distributor to the book trade in the United States and Canada:

Rizzoli International Publications, Inc.
597 Fifth Avenue
New York, NY 10017

Distributor to the art trade in the United States:

Letraset USA
40 Eisenhower Drive
Paramus, NJ 07653

Distributor to the art trade in Canada:

Letraset Canada Limited
555 Alden Road
Markham, Ontario L3R 3L5, Canada

Distributed throughout the rest of the world by:

Hearst Books International
105 Madison Avenue
New York, NY 10016

Library of Congress Cataloging-in-Publication Data

Great menu graphics / by the editors of PBC
International, Inc.
       p.   cm.
   Includes index.
   ISBN 0-86636-106-5
    1. Menu design. 2. Graphic arts. I. PBC International.
NC1002.M4G74 1989
769.5—dc 19   88-39185
                                     CIP

Typesetting by McFarland Graphics, Inc.
Printing and binding by Toppan Printing
Co. (H.K.) Ltd.

PRINTED IN HONG KONG
10 9 8 7 6 5 4 3 2 1

Contents

Introduction

Dining out has become a modern obsession. As the food
service business soars on the currents of the dual-career
family, increasing affluence and heightened sophistication
about food, menus have gained steadily in the estimation of
both the public and professional restaurateurs.
As a promotional vehicle for the restaurant, and as an art
form, menus present a new frontier. As the pieces in this
book demonstrate, there are virtually no limits on what can be
achieved, both esthetically and in a marketing sense.
This surge of interest in food, and in menus, has resulted in
an increase in the number of entries in contests for
excellence in menu design, and in the number of publications
featuring excellent menus. In this book, we have carefully
selected the most innovative, well-planned, and attractive
menus. These pieces prove that, far from being a financial
drain on a restaurant, great menus can be a wise investment.
This collection of menus has been organized by type of eating
establishment and by type of menu for easy reference. In the
interviews in this book, professionals representing
every sector of food service explain what elements they
consider when evaluating a menu and what makes a menu
work best for their segment of the business. The directories
cross-reference restaurants, menu design and production
firms, menu designers, artists, illustrators, photographers,
printers and paper suppliers.
We hope the menus, and this detailed reference information,
will present the designer, the restaurateur, and the menu
collector a true feast of ideas about menus and menu design.
Bon appetit!

Theme Menus

Theme restaurants have become very popular in the last two
decades. A theme restaurant is one which has chosen to
emphasize a single element of decor or design, and has made
that element its central motif. For example, the railroad station
is a popular theme. A menu showing old photographs,
prints of trains, and listing items in railroad terms carries
through the theme.

There's no limit on what can be done with theme menus, and
of all categories, this one offers the greatest scope for
spontaneity and whimsical imagination.

Restaurant: Humpty Dumpty

Location: Phoenix, Arizona

Designer: David Bartels

Firm: Bartels & Company

Illustrator: Gary Overacre

Humpty Dumpty is a family-oriented restaurant and coffee shop. The menu's fare has a complete array of breakfast, lunch, and dinner selections, for a light repas to a full meal. The dessert menu is on the back.

Restaurant: Take Five
Location: Louisville, Kentucky
Designer: Lew Lehrman
Firm: Design Unlimited/Culinary Concepts
Illustrator: Robin Smith
Printer: East Coast Lithographers
Die-Cutter: Freedman Cutouts
Specifications:
Paper: Carolina Coated Cover
Size: 10¼″ x 13¼″

Now the patron can be the director with this die-cut moveable clapboard menu. The letter "A" doubles as a movie camera. A silhouetted film clip of a dramatic love scene unfolds at the top of the page. The inside entry descriptions reinforce the movie theme.

Restaurant: T.G.I. Friday's

Location: Nationwide chain headquartered in Dallas, Texas

Designer: Woody Pirtle

Firm: The Richards Group

Illustrator: Bill Jenkins

Printer: Heritage Press

Specifications: T.G.I. Friday's Summer Watermelon Menu

Size: 6¼″ x 17″ cover

What better way to set the tone for a summer meal than with this menu from T.G.I. Friday's? Opening to a luscious cross-section of a watermelon that looks good enough to eat, this menu offers an array of garden-fresh salads and iced drinks. And what do you do with the watermelon seeds? Incorporate them into the design, of course!

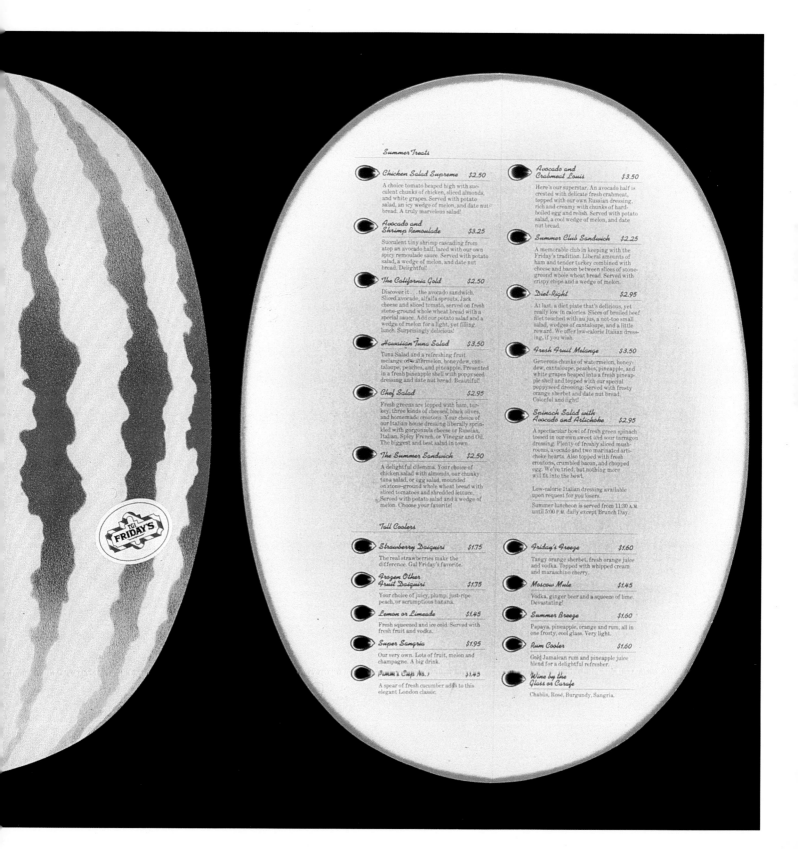

Restaurant: Dalt's
Location: Nationwide chain owned by T.G.I. Friday's, Inc., headquartered in Dallas, Texas
Designer: Woody Pirtle
Firm: Pirtle Design
Illustrator: Ken Shafer
Printer: Allcraft Printing
Specifications: Dalt's Summer Menu
Size: 6¼″ x 14″
Paper: Kimdura

The fountain on the cover is delightfully refreshing. Dalt's summer menu gives the reader the feeling of coolness with its sandy browns and wavy lines suggestive of water. Even the food category headings, which all use the word summer, have a cooling effect.

SUMMER SOUP AND SPECIALS

Chilled Gazpacho Soup A refreshing, homemade, crunchy Spanish blend of fresh tomatoes, cucumbers, bell peppers, celery and carrots with a hint of lemon and spices. $1.95
With half of a Dalts club sandwich and warm, homemade potato chips. $3.75

Seafood Nachos Crisp tortilla chips topped with warm langostinos (a taste between shrimp and lobster), cool sour cream and green onions, all covered with melted Jack cheese and sliced Jalapenos. $4.95

Homemade Potato Chips A basketful of warm, homemade, skin-on potato chips, seasoned and served with sour cream and chives for dipping. $1.50

Loaded Potato Chips Homemade, warm, specially seasoned skin-on potato chips loaded with melted cheddar cheese and crumbled bacon. Served with sour cream and chives for dipping. $2.50

Summer Enchilada A flour tortilla filled with a light blend of chicken, mushrooms, green chilies and lime, then topped with a mild creamy sauce and melted cheddar and Jack cheeses. Served with a wedge of melon and warm, homemade potato chips. $4.25

Dalts Taquitos Four hot and crisp tortilla rolls; two filled with chicken breast, and two with beef. All are also filled with mixed cheeses, green onions and spices and are topped with melted cheese. Served with homemade salsa, guacamole and sour cream for dipping. $4.95

Chimisalachanga™ A large flour tortilla rolled and filled with avocado, cheddar and Jack cheeses, tomatoes, lettuce and Parsley Chicken Salad. Fried hot and crispy outside, but cool inside. Served with salsa, a wedge of melon and warm, homemade potato chips. $5.50

Seafood Kabob A light, summer kabob of large shrimp, scallops and mushroom caps charbroiled and basted with a honey, butter and lime sauce. Served with a wedge of melon and warm, homemade potato chips. $6.95

SUMMER SANDWICH PLATES

Baguette Sandwich A long French loaf, halved, scooped and heated until crisp for a classic light crusty sandwich. Your choice of:

Parsley Chicken Salad with lettuce and tomato. $4.25

Albacore Tuna Salad with lettuce and tomato. $4.25

Ham, bacon, provolone and Swiss cheeses with Dijon mustard. $4.75

All served with a wedge of melon, warm, homemade potato chips, and pepperoncinis.

Dalts Summer Sandwich Stone-ground whole wheat bread piled high with homemade Albacore Tuna Salad or Parsley Chicken Salad, lettuce and tomato. Served with a wedge of melon and warm, homemade potato chips. $3.95

Charbroiled Chicken Breast Sandwich Tender chicken breast marinated in a butter, lime and wine sauce, then charbroiled for flavor. Served on a sesame seed bun with a wedge of melon and warm, homemade potato chips. $4.25

SUMMER SALAD PLATES

Fresh Fruit Platter with Cottage Cheese Large cut chunks of fresh cantaloupe, watermelon, seedless grapes, pineapple, honeydew melon, bananas and strawberries surrounding fresh, cool cottage cheese. Served with warm pita wedges and your choice of raisin cream dressing or poppyseed dressing for dipping. $4.95

Confetti Pasta Salad Red, green, and white (tomato, spinach, and egg) pasta shells tossed with mushrooms, pimentos, black olives, peas, artichoke hearts and cucumbers in a tangy olive oil dressing. Served with cheddar cheese toast and a wedge of melon. $3.95

Greek Salad Mixed lettuce greens topped with diced tomatoes, cucumbers, feta cheese, red onions, Greek olives, and pepperoncinis, all surrounded by warm, crisp pita wedges. Served with a tangy olive oil and lemon dressing. $4.50

Stuffed Avocado A Calavo avocado half stuffed with homemade Albacore Tuna Salad or Parsley Chicken Salad and served with a wedge of melon, crisp pita wedges, and warm, homemade potato chips. $3.95

Langostino Louis Tender langostinos (a taste between shrimp and lobster) mounded on greens and surrounded by an avocado half, egg wedges, thick-sliced tomatoes and black olives. Served with Thousand Island dressing. $6.95

SUMMER DESSERT

Fruit Pizza A light cookie crust layered with cream cheese and topped with colorful pineapple, kiwi, bananas, strawberries, mandarin oranges and pecans. All laced with an apricot-rum glaze. By the slice. $2.50

SUMMER DRINKS

One-Free-Hour-in-the-Candy-Store A creamy chocolate cherry almond surprise.

Tutti-Frutti Life Saver A mellow, fruity drink with two liqueurs and three juices.

Banana Nutbread A creamy, nutty banana treat.

Long Island Iced Tea A blend of four liqueurs and the surprising taste of iced tea.

White Sangria Light and tingly white wine drink with fresh citrus juices.

Amaretto Choco-Cream A creamy blend with amaretto and dark creme de cacao.

Citrus Rum Cooler Light rum, triple sec and fresh juices.

Flamingo Fresh, bright, tart flavor with pineapple, coconut and sloe gin.

Banana Popsicle Creamy, cool banana flavor.

Lynchburg Lemonade A Jack Daniels lemonade with added zip.

Mexican Runner Like a tangy, frozen, strawberry tart with two liqueurs, tequila, strawberries and rum.

Restaurant: Joe's Corner
Location: Philadelphia, Pennsylvania
Designer: Myron Wasserman
Firm: Myron Wasserman's Studio
Illustrators: David and Fred Karge,
Karge Twin Studios
Printer: Pearl Pressman Liberty
Specifications:
Size: 10″ x 14″ cover
Paper: Kromecoat

The airbrush illustration on the cover shows front and rear views of Joe Frazier's boxing robe. The typography on the back of the robe is the logo of the restaurant. The menu copy is written in boxing terms. Enjoyable for the family—and boxing fans, of course.

Restaurant: Joe's Corner
Location: Philadelphia, Pennsylvania
Designer: Myron Wasserman
Firm: Myron Wasserman's Studio
Illustrators: David and Fred Karge,
Karge Twin Studios
Printer: Pearl Pressman Liberty
Specifications:
Size: 10″ x 14″ cover
Paper: Kromecoat

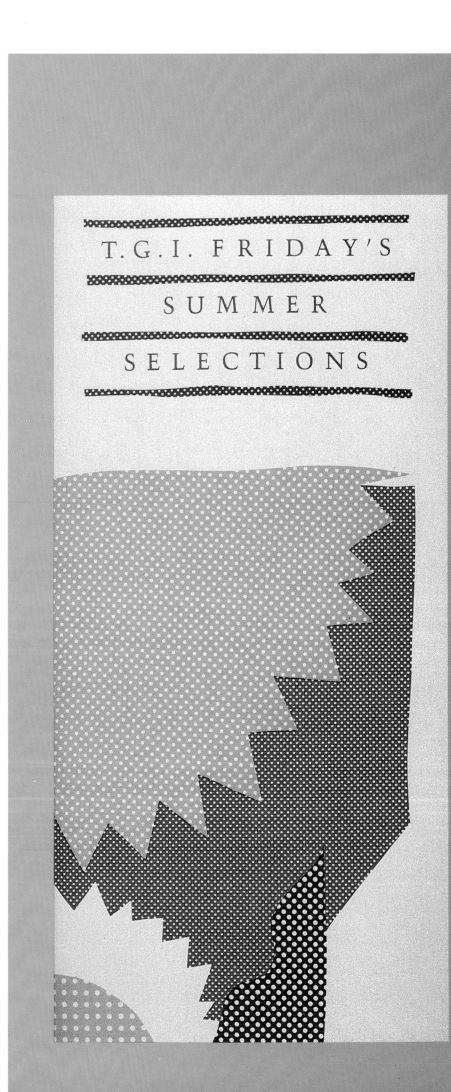

Restaurant: T.G.I. Friday's
Location: Nationwide chain headquartered in Dallas, Texas
Designer: Woody Pirtle
Firm: Pirtle Design
Illustrators: Woody Pirtle and Luis Acevedo
Printer: Allcraft Printing
Specifications: T.G.I. Friday's Summer Selections
Size: 5″ x 10⅜″

The patchwork quilt design of this summer menu creates a mood of homey serenity. The lovely summer poem by William Motherwell suggests idyllic memories of childhood.

THEY COME! THE MERRY SUMMER MONTHS

They come! the merry summer months of
  beauty, song, and flowers;
They come! the gladsome months that bring
  thick leafiness to bowers.
Up, up, my heart! and walk abroad; fling cark
  and care aside;
Seek silent hills, or rest thyself where peaceful
  waters glide;
Or, underneath the shadow vast of patriarchal
  tree,
Scan through its leaves the cloudless sky in
  rapt tranquility.
                 — *William Motherwell.*

T.G.I. FRIDAY'S   CULINARY   IMPRESSIONS

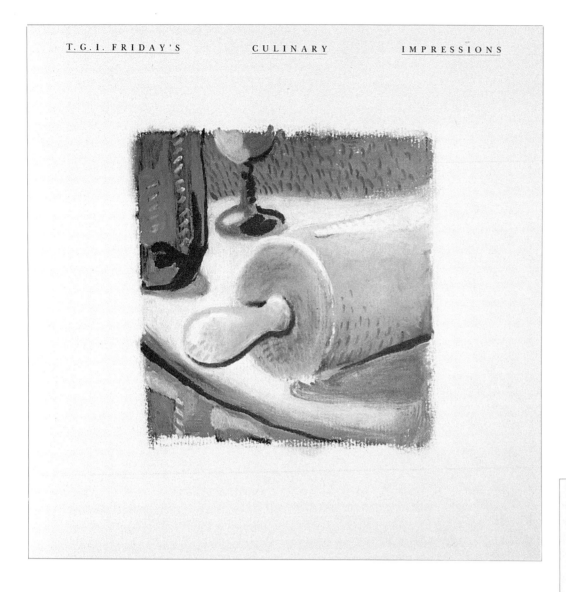

SPECIAL BRUNCH DRIN

RAMOS GIN FIZZ
*A delicate, frothy combination of lemon, light cream,
white and gin topped with the aroma of flowers.*

BRANDY MILK PUNCH
*The combination of brandy, dark cocoa and milk wi
hint of sweetness.*

MIMOSAS
*Fresh orange, lemon or lime juices with sparkling
champagne over crushed ice.*

GRAND MIMOSA
A fresh orange mimosa accented with Grand Marnie

CHAMPAGNE BRUNCH
*A tingly, creamy blend of pina colada, yogurt, champ
Grand Marnier and orange sherbet.*

SILVER MERCEDES
*Refreshing cranberry juice and vodka blended with a
sherbet and poured into champagne.*

CALIFORNIA DOMESTIC CHAMPAGNE

TGI FRIDAY'S ALL AMERICAN SMOOTHIES
An all natural frozen fruit drink.

Andre the Peach Lifter	*Gold Medalist*
Blueberry Triathlon	*Los Angeles Banana*
Coco Nut Climber	*Tropical Runner*

Restaurant: T.G.I. Friday's
Location: Nationwide chain headquartered in
Dallas, Texas
Designer: Woody Pirtle
Firm: Pirtle Design
Illustrator: Woody Pirtle
Printer: Allcraft Printing
Specifications: T.G.I. Friday's Culinary Impressions
Size: 9" x 9"

The beautiful impressionistic paintings on this menu
are suitable for framing, and Friday's sells the
menus as retail items for that purpose. As menu art,
they are appetizing and sensual and set the stage for
the dining experience.

UNCH CROISSANTS

*al Friday's size tender flaky croissants, halved, filled
eggs and other fresh ingredients. Served with break-
otatoes and fruit salad.*

ISSANT BENEDICT/$7.50
*hed eggs with Canadian bacon and topped with
ndaise sauce.*

ISSANT SARDOU/$7.50
*hed eggs with creamed spinach, artichoke bottoms and
d with hollandaise sauce.*

ISSANT OSCAR/$8.50
*hed eggs with sauteed crabmeat, asparagus and
d with hollandaise sauce.*

ISSANT TENDERLOIN BENEDICT/$8.25
*hed eggs with sliced filet, sauteed mushrooms and
d with hollandaise sauce.*

ISSANT HAM & EGG WITH HOLLANDAISE/$7.50
*mbled eggs with sauteed ham, cheddar cheese and
d with hollandaise sauce.*

ISSANT BACON, MUSHROOM & EGGS/$7.50
*mbled eggs with sauteed mushrooms, cheddar, crisp
n and topped with melted cheddar cheese.*

combination of two available.

RADITIONAL QUICHES

*riday's Recommendation, Fresh baked
che in our main menu.*

PLATE 1
CROISSANT SARDOU

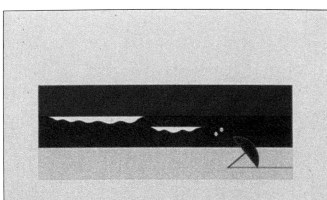

Restaurant: T.G.I. Friday's
Location: Nationwide chain headquartered in Dallas, Texas
Designer: Woody Pirtle
Firm: Pirtle Design
Illustrators: Woody Pirtle and David Kampa
Printer: Allcraft Printing
Specifications: T.G.I. Friday's Summer 1983 Menu
Size: 7⁵⁄₁₆″ x 12½″
Paper: Kimdura

The painting on this award-winning menu depicts a tranquil summer scene on the beach. Elegant and simple, the art is harmoniously accented by solid colored pages within the menu, using the four colors of the painting throughout. Clearly written descriptive copy is printed in two colors.

SUMMER SANDWICH PLATES

Baguette Sandwiches
A long French loaf, halved, scooped, flattened and heated until crisp for a classic light and crisp sandwich. Your choice of:

Ham, bacon, provolone and Swiss cheese with Dijon mustard. $6.25

Turkey, bacon, provolone cheese, lettuce and tomato with Dijon mustard. $5.95

Poor Boy of ham, salami, provolone and Swiss cheese, lettuce and tomato, with Italian dressing. $6.45

Bacon, lettuce and tomato with mayonnaise. $5.75

All served with a fresh fruit kabob, poppyseed dressing, warm, homemade potato chips and peppercorns.

Charbroiled Chicken Breast Sandwich
Tender chicken breast marinated in a butter, lime and wine sauce and charbroiled for flavor. Served on a sesame seed bun with a fresh fruit kabob, poppyseed dressing and warm, homemade potato chips. $4.95

Turkey-Avocado-Bacon-Jack Cheese Croissant
A Friday's-size croissant filled with turkey breast, bacon, Jack cheese, sliced avocado and a special mustard dressing. Served with a jewel salad and poppyseed dressing. $6.95

Mediterranean Tuna Melt
Mediterranean style tuna salad on thin, toasted pita bread and topped with melted Jack cheese. Served with warm, homemade potato chips and a wedge of melon. $4.75

Turkey Asparagus Melt
Cool asparagus spears wrapped with turkey breast and topped with melted Swiss cheese and alfalfa sprouts on stone-ground whole wheat bread. Served with warm, homemade potato chips and a wedge of melon. $4.75

Bacon-Mushroom-Guacamole Sandwich
Stone-ground whole wheat bread mounded with sautéed mushrooms, crisp bacon, guacamole, alfalfa sprouts and melted Jack cheese. Served with warm, homemade potato chips and a wedge of melon. $4.50

Baguette Burger
Friday's hamburger, rolled in onions, specially shaped, charbroiled, and covered with melted Swiss cheese. Served on a light, crusty French loaf. Plate $5.25 or Platter (with homemade wedge fries and a large Friday's onion ring). $5.75

SUMMER SALADS

Fresh Fruit Platter with Cottage Cheese
Large cut chunks of fresh cantaloupe, watermelon, seedless grapes, pineapple, honeydew melon, bananas and strawberries surrounding fresh, light cottage cheese. Served with poppyseed dressing and warm, crisp pita wedges. $5.45

Papaya and Salad
A fresh papaya half with a strawberry and lime wedge, accompanied by your choice of one of the following: Chicken Salad with White Grapes, or Mediterranean Tuna Salad, or Shrimp and Snow Pea Salad. Served with warm, homemade potato chips and crisp pita wedges. $5.95

Confetti Pasta Salad
Red, green, and white (tomato, spinach, and egg) pasta shells tossed with mushrooms, pimentos, black olives, peas, artichoke hearts and cucumbers in a tangy olive oil dressing. Served with cheddar cheese toast and a fresh fruit kabob with poppyseed dressing. $5.95

Greek Salad
Mixed lettuce greens topped with diced tomatoes, cucumbers, feta cheese, red onions, Greek olives and pepperoncini, all surrounded by warm, crisp pita wedges. Served with a tangy olive oil and lemon dressing. $5.25

Block Island Seafood Salad
Shrimp, crabmeat and whitefish tossed with yogurt-caper dressing and mounded on lettuce. Surrounded with egg slices, tomato wedges, warm, homemade potato chips and crisp pita wedges. $7.95

Langostino Louis
Tender langostinos (tails) between shrimp and lobster) mounded on greens and surrounded by egg wedges, thick-sliced tomatoes and black olives. Served with Thousand Island dressing. $7.95

SUMMER DESSERT

Fruit Pizza
A light cookie crust layered with cream cheese and topped with colorful pineapple, kiwi, bananas, strawberries, mandarin oranges and pears. All laced with an apricot-rum glaze. By the slice, $2.50

Restaurant: T.G.I. Friday's
Location: Nationwide chain headquartered in
Dallas, Texas
Designer: Woody Pirtle
Firm: Pirtle Design
Illustrator: Woody Pirtle
Printer: Allcraft Printing
Specifications: T.G.I. Friday's Culinary Impressions
Size: 9″ x 9″

Restaurant: The Maestro
Location: New York, New York
Designer: Jane Barbara
Firm: Menu Makers Plus
Illustrator: Jane Barbara
Printer: Menu Makers Plus
Specifications:
Size: 7″ x 10″
Paper: Kromecoat

The Maestro, located near Lincoln Center, specializes in continental cuisine. The owner of the restaurant is a musician, and during Sunday brunch and dinner hours, he and other restaurant staff members entertain clients with live music—from Bach to Broadway. The menu design conveys the idea of celebration as well as formal elegance.

Restaurant: T.G.I. Friday's
Location: Nationwide chain headquartered in Dallas, Texas
Designer: Woody Pirtle
Firm: The Richards Group
Illustrators: Don Grimes and Bob Dennard
Calligrapher: Don Grimes
Printer: Heritage Press
Specifications: T.G.I. Friday's Spiral Menu
Size: 8½″ x 11″

T.G.I. Friday's spiral menu was one of the first menus to delight the chain's loyal clientele. Printed over a decade ago, this was a departure from the "traditional" menu form. The cover, designed like a school composition book, opens to handwritten entries, complete with doodles and comments in the margin.

Menu

Lunch

Dinner

Drinks

Sit back and enjoy a lunch hour layover in our comfortable surroundings. We've got something for every appetite and every craving: homemade soups, fresh salads, mountainous sandwiches and station master specialties. For passengers on a tight schedule, we offer the noon express.

Whether you've been working on the railroad, the yard or your "in" basket, you deserve to treat yourself and your tastebuds to dinner at the station. We specialize in choice steaks and fresh seafood flown in from Alaska, Canada and the Gulf of Mexico. And all you have to do is cross the tracks.

All aboard the bar car for a rollicking ride in Cahoots (our downstairs bar), our upstairs main bar or the dining room. We've got a trainload of imported beers, cordials, hot coffee concoctions and station creations. Our wine list is rather impressive too. We even have a three hour happy hour.

Restaurant and Bar
333 First Street South
Minneapolis, MN 55401
339-3339

FIRST STREET STATION

RESTAURANT AND BAR

Drinks

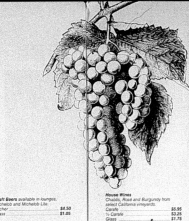

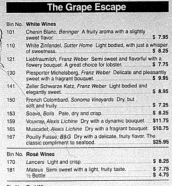

The Bar Car

Bar Highballs (ex: Tom Collins, Bloody Mary)	$1.95
Call Highballs (ex: Chivas and water, Canadian Club and Coke)	$2.50
Bar Cocktails (ex: Martini, Manhattan)	$2.65
Call Cocktails (ex: Beefeater Martini, Tanqueray Gimlet)	$2.95
Tropical Cocktails (ex: Mai Tai, Long Island Iced Tea)	$2.95
After Dinner Cocktails (ex: Black Russian, Rusty Nail)	$3.00
Premium Cocktails (ex: Stolichnaya Black Russian)	$3.50
Ice Cream Drinks (featuring Häagen-Dazs ice cream)	$3.50
Coffee and Hot Drinks (ex: Irish Coffee, Hot Buttered Rum)	$2.95

The Whistle Stop Happy Hour

Monday - Friday, 4-7 p.m. (an actual *three* hour happy hour!)
Featuring ½ price drinks, highballs, cocktails, wine and domestic beers.
Get fresh at our happy hour seafood bar: Oysters $.25 each, Shrimp
$.25 each. Or choose anything from our "Early Arrival" appetizers (see
Dinner menu). Ask your waiter or waitress about our summer and
winter drink creations.

The Grain Train

Sample the brew of a different country every day for only $1.15. (All
imports regularly $1.95, except for Foster's, a 25 ounce can for $2.75.)

Heineken (Holland)	**Monday**
Molson Golden (Canada)	**Tuesday**
Moosehead (Canada)	**Wednesday**
Dortmunder Union (Germany)	**Thursday**
St. Pauli Girl Light or Dark (Germany)	**Friday**
Foster's Lager (Australia)	**(not on special)**
Bass Ale (Great Britian)	**(not on special)**

Domestic Beers *Miller High Life, Miller Lite, Budweiser, Pabst Blue
Ribbon and Heileman's Special Export* $1.25

The Cordial Caboose Liqueurs served straight up or on rocks $2.75

Amaretto Almond flavored liqueur from Italy.
Baileys Irish Cream Cream liqueur with a rich toffee flavor.
Benedictine Secret herb and cognac formula from a Benedictine monk.
B & B Dry, spicy formula of brandy and Benedictine.
Chartreuse Yellow or green herb liqueur of the Carthusian monks.
Cointreau Orange flavored liqueur from France.
Drambuie Scotch based, honey flavored liqueur.
Galliano Licorice flavored liqueur from Italy.
Grand Marnier Orange flavored cognac liqueur.
Irish Mist Honey and herb liqueur from Ireland.
Kahlua Coffee flavored liqueur from Mexico.
Metaxa 7 Star Brandy based liqueur from Greece.
Pernod Anise flavored liqueur from France.
Tia Maria Coffee flavored liqueur from Jamaica.
Vandermint Chocolate mint liqueur from Holland.

The Cognac Collection These fine brandies, known for their
smoothness and heady, dry aroma, are produced exclusively in the
Cognac region of France.

Courvoisier VS, Martell VS	$2.75
Courvoisier VSOP, Hennessy VS, Remy Martin VSOP	$2.95

*Happy hour prices available in
lounges only.*

Draft Beers *available in lounges,
Michelob and Michelob Lite.*

Pitcher	$4.50
Glass	$1.05

House Wines *Chablis, Rosé and Burgundy from
select California vineyards.*

Carafe	$5.95
½ Carafe	$3.25
Glass	$1.75

The Grape Escape

Bin No. White Wines

101	Chenin Blanc, *Beringer* A fruity aroma with a slightly sweet flavor.	$ 7.95
110	White Zinfandel, *Sutter Home* Light bodied, with just a whisper of sweetness.	$ 8.25
121	Liebfraumilch, *Franz Weber* Semi sweet and flavorful with a flowery bouquet. A great choice for lobster.	$ 7.75
130	Piesporter Michelsberg, *Franz Weber* Delicate and pleasantly sweet with a fragrant bouquet.	$ 9.95
141	Zeller Schwarze Katz, *Franz Weber* Light bodied and elegantly sweet.	$ 8.95
150	French Colombard, *Sonoma Vineyards* Dry, but soft and fruity.	$ 7.25
153	Soave, *Bolla* Pale, dry and crisp.	$ 8.25
159	Vouvray, *Alexis Lichine* Dry with a dynamic bouquet.	$11.75
165	Muscadet, *Alexis Lichine* Dry with a fragrant bouquet.	$10.75
167	Pouilly Fuisse, *B&G* Dry with a delicate, fruity flavor. The classic compliment to seafood.	$25.95

Bin No. Rosé Wines

170	*Lancers* Light and crisp.	$ 8.25
181	*Mateus* Semi sweet with a light, fruity taste.	$ 7.75
	½ Bottle	$ 4.75

Bin No. Red Wines

190	Beaujolais, *Louis Jadot* Dry, but fruit filled and fresh.	$ 9.95
201	Cabernet Sauvignon, *Inglenook, Estate Bottled* Dry, rich and full bodied.	$11.95
210	Zinfandel, *Inglenook, Estate Bottled* Dry and full bodied with a raspberry aroma.	$ 7.95
218	Gamay Beaujolais, *Inglenook, Estate Bottled* Fruity and dry with a special charm.	$ 8.25
221	Mouton Cadet Red, *Rothschild* A masterful dry Bordeaux. Try it with any of our steaks.	$10.50
	½ Bottle	$ 5.75
230	Chateauneuf du Pape, *B & G* Rich and full bodied with a spicy flavor.	$16.25
241	Valpolicella, *Bolla* Fresh and light bodied with a dry aftertaste.	$ 8.25
250	Lambrusco, *Giacobazzi* Sweet and slightly effervescent.	$ 6.50
256	St. Emilon, *B & G* Full bodied and dry with a powerful bouquet.	$14.50

Bin No. Champagne

261	Moet Et Chandon, *Dom Perignon*	$79.95
270	Cordon Rouge, *Mumm's, Vintage*	$39.95
281	Extra Dry, *Mumm's, Non-Vintage*	$29.95
	½ Bottle	$16.25
290	Extra Dry, *Korbel*	$12.95

*Ask us for the scoop on dome specials,
including hors d'oeuvres and drink
specials to celebrate the thrill of victory
and the agony of defeat. (Specials good
before and after the games.)*

*Locomotives like these used to drive into
the First Street Station for repair in the
mid 1900s. In fact, the railroad tracks
are still beneath our floors.*

*The uncomfortable train rides of bygone
days took their toll on weary
travelers...or was it happy hour in the
bar car?*

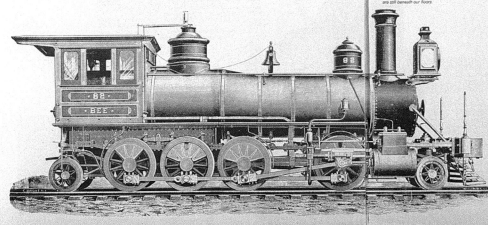

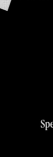

Restaurant: First Street Station
Location: Minneapolis, Minnesota
Designer: James Nancekivell
Firm: Krogstad Design Associates, Inc.
Specifications:
Size: 18½″ x 22″
Paper: Carnival Offset Vellum

This menu is designed as three menus in one:
lunch, dinner, and beverage. The railroad theme is
carried throughout in the look as well as in the
written copy. In the drink section, the photographs
re-create an old-fashioned bar car. The entries are
headed with catchy phrases like "Bar Car," "The
Whistle Stop," "Happy Hour," "The Grain Train,"
and the "Grape Escape." The colors are the brown
of old railroad ties and steely blue-gray. The written
copy is very descriptive and humorous.

Restaurant: T.G.I. Friday's
Location: Nationwide chain headquartered in Dallas, Texas
Designers: Luis Acevedo and Woody Pirtle
Firm: Pirtle Design
Illustrator: Luis Acevedo
Printer: Allcraft Printing
Specifications: T.G.I. Friday's Dictionary
Size: 7″ x 9½″

This early menu was modeled after a dictionary. With gold-foil stamping on a red leatherette cover, the menu opens to an alphabetical index, just like a real dictionary. With entries as the words, and their descriptions as the definitions, T.G.I. Friday's is cleverly educating their clientele. On this sample page of their wine list, they have provided the correct pronunciation, wine region, and a full description of the type of wine and its flavor.

WINES

Aa

California White

Char·don·nay (ˌshär-dō-ˈnā) n. **1.** A Geyser Peak, Alexander Valley wine. **2.** A clear, crisp, dry and fruity wine. $8.95

Pi·not Char·don·nay (pē-ˈnō ˌshär-dō-ˈnā) n. **1.** A Beaulieu Vineyards, Napa Valley wine. **2.** A very dry, straw gold and extremely flavorful wine. $10.95

Dry Sau·vig·non Blanc (drī ˈso-vin- ya ˈblä) n. **1.** A Beaulieu Vineyards Napa Valley wine. **2.** A dry wine with a delicate roundness. **3.** A wine comparable to a white Bordeaux. $9.95

Cha·blis (ˈshäb-lē) n. **1.** A wine from the Beaulieu Vineyards, Estate. **2.** A light, dry and very pleasant wine. $7.25

Che·nin·Blanc (ˈshä-nän ˈblä) n. **1.** A Beringer wine. **2.** A fresh and fruity wine with a hint of sweetness. $7.75

California Red

Cab·er·net Sau·vig·non (ˈcab-ˌaōr-nä ˈsō-vin-ˌya) n. **1.** A Beaulieu Vineyards, Napa Valley, Beau Tour wine. **2.** A mellow and fruity wine. $8.95

Zin·fan·del (ˈzin-ˌfan-del) n. **1.** A Sebastiani Vineyards, Sonoma wine. **2.** A pleasantly soft, dry and fruity wine. $6.95

German White

Pies·port·er Gold·tröpf·chen Kab·i·nett (ˈpēz-port-ər gōldt-ˈtröepf-ˌkien ˈkab-i-ˌnet) n. A medium dry wine with the captivating bouquet of the Riesling grape. $8.50

Be·reich Mo·selle (ˈbair-rysh mō-zel′) n. **1.** A Deinhard Green Label wine. **2.** A wine with an extremely delicate bouquet, balanced by a pleasant crispness. $7.95

Lieb·frau·milch (ˈlēp-frou-ˌmilk) n. **1.** A Riesling wine with the Blue Nun label. **2.** A semi-dry, fruity, fresh wine. $8.50

The Cabernet Sauvignon grape (red)

WINES

French White

Ma·con Vil·lages (mä-ˈkōn ˈvil-ijs) n. **1.** Wine from Bouchard Pére & Fils. **2.** Wine from the Pinot Chardonnay grape. **3.** A fresh, fruity, dry and somewhat complex wine. $11.95

Ge·wurz·tram·in·er (gə-ˈvyrts-ˌträ-mi-nər) n. **1.** An Alsatian wine produced by the Trimbach family. **2.** A fairly dry and crisp wine which tastes like a spicy German wine. $10.95

French Red

Beau·jo·lais Vil·lage (bō′shə-ˌlä ˈvil-ij) n. A wine with a fresh, light, fruity flavor and aroma. $9.50

Bor·deaux (bor-ˈdō) n. **1.** The wine of Chateau Larose-Trintaudon Haut Medoc. **2.** A full-bodied and elegant claret. $11.95

Rosé

Ma·teus (ma-ˈtüs) n. A medium dry wine with a light flavor. $7.50

Italian Red

Chi·an·ti Clas·si·co (kē-ˈän,te ˈkläs-ē-kō) n. **1.** A wine from the house of Cella. **2.** A light bodied, fresh and fruity wine. $6.95

Lam·brus·co (läm-ˈbroōs-kō) n. **1.** A wine produced by Riunite. **2.** A pleasantly sweet and tingly wine. $6.25

Italian White

Soa·ve (ˈswä-ve) n. **1.** A wine from the Bolla Co. **2.** A light and refreshing white wine. **3.** A very dry wine. $7.95

Or·vi·e·to (ˌor-vē-ˈä-tō) n. **1.** An Abboccato (semi-dry) wine produced by Ruffino. **2.** A medium dry, light and fresh wine. $7.50

House Wine (ˈhaüs ˈwin) n. **1.** A selected California premium wine by the liter, ½ liter or glass. **2.** A Burgundy, Chablis, or Rosé.

"FRI·DAY'S" Home·made San·gria (ˈfrid-ēz ˈhōm-ˌmäd san-ˈgre-ə) n. **1.** A red or white fruity wine punch. **2.** A wine drink served by the pitcher or glass.

WINES
continued

The Pinot Chardonnay grape (white)

The Gamay grape (red)

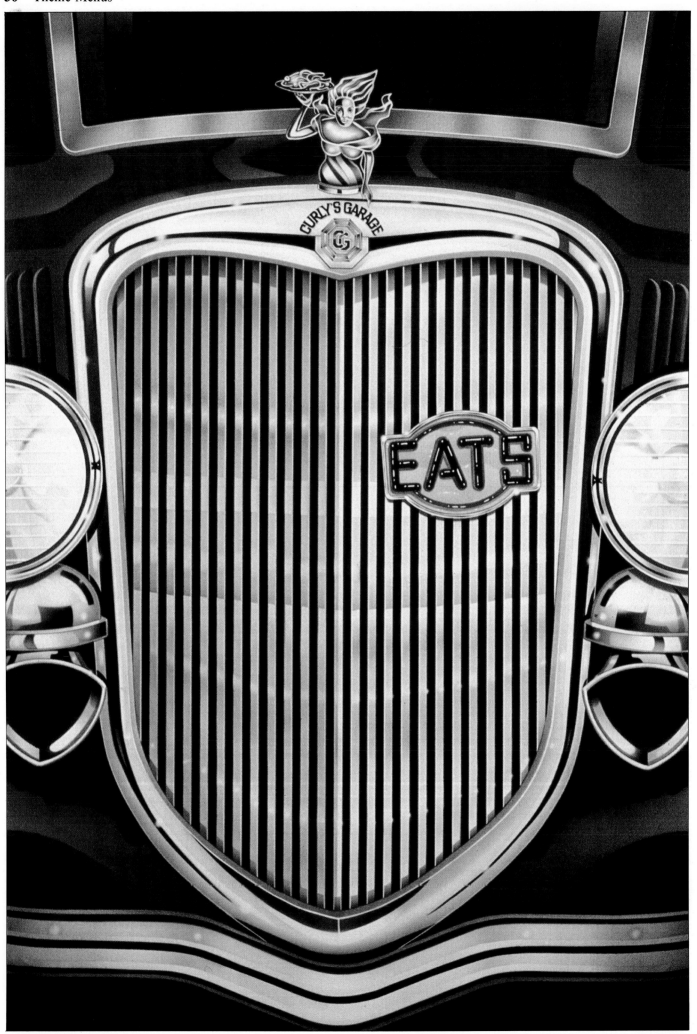

Restaurant:	Curly's Garage
Location:	Charlottesville, Virginia
Designer:	Myron Wasserman
Firm:	Myron Wasserman's Studio
Illustrator:	Tony Mascio
Printer:	Pearl Pressman Liberty
Specifications:	
Size:	10″ x 14″
Paper:	Kromecoat

The restaurant's theme, a 1930's style auto garage, is oriented toward families and college students with its moderately priced food selection. The airbrush illustration on the cover is a real showstopper. Notice the hood ornament, a goddess-like spirit lady carrying a tray of food. On the back of the menu is an aerial view of a place setting; the wineglass strangely resembles a car's backlight. The restaurant's interior is adorned with antique car parts; in the foyer is an actual 1934 Ford on a lift.

Restaurant: Cafe Fanny
Location: New York, New York
Designer: Milton Glaser
Firm: Milton Glaser, Inc.
Photographer: Henry Wolf
Printer: Metropolitan Printing
Specifications: Dinner Menu, Supper Menu, and Breakfast Mat
Size: 6" x 13" dinner menu; 4½" x 6" supper menu; 13½" x 10" breakfast mat
Paper: Mohawk Superfine Cover

This restaurant was created by George Lang for the Biltmore Hotel in the spirit of a fine, Old World Viennese cafe, replete with savory delicacies and a splendid range of confections. Its handsomly crafted detailing, antique fixtures, and rich finishing materials created a genuinely distinguished and grand atmosphere. Business people, before- and after-theater crowds, hotel guests, and late-nighters were among its clientele. The photographs are imaginative re-creations of the renowned Viennese ballerina Fanny Elssler, in a variety of poses. The photographs were to be used as a decorative element in the restaurant, which unfortunately closed before that part of the design could be implemented.

THE CONTINENTAL

Juice, Jam, Toast and Coffee , Tea or Milk 2.60

THE CAFE SPECIAL

French Fruit Compote Croissant or Warm Danish Pastry
Coffee , Tea or Milk 3.30

FRUITS AND JUICES

½ Grapefruit or Orange Sections 1.60
Chilled Melon (in season) 1.60
Stewed Prunes 1.60
Sliced Bananas in Cream 1.50
Freshly Squeezed Orange Juice . . . . *large* 1.65 *small* 1.10
Tomato Juice . . . . *large* 1.65 *small* 1.10
Berries (in season) served with cream 1.60

EGG DISHES *All egg dishes served with toast and preserves*

Single Egg, soft-boiled, poached or fried 1.25
Two Eggs, any style 2.30
Fried Egg with Ham, Bacon or Sausage 2.45
Two Eggs, any style with Ham, Bacon or Sausage 3.50
Plain Omelette 2.70
Omelette Stuffed with Muenster Cheese 3.20
Ham Omelette 3.50
Omelette with Jelly 2.95

FROM THE GRILL

An Order of Bacon or Link Sausage 2.30
Broiled Ham 2.30
Steak & Egg 5.75

CEREALS

Oatmeal 1.40
Cream of Wheat 1.40
Crisp Cereals with Milk or Cream 1.40

COFFEE PASTRIES

MONDAY
Apricot Pastry Fanny
Butter Danish Filled with Double Apricot Butter

TUESDAY
Lekvar Pastry
Butter Danish Filled with Hungarian Prune Jam

WEDNESDAY
Pineapple Cheese Roll
Butter Danish with Cream Cheese and Pineapple Filling

THURSDAY
Almond Cream Slice Jalousie
Puff Pastry Filled with Almond Paste

FRIDAY, SATURDAY & SUNDAY
Double Raspberry Pastry
Butter Danish Filled with Double Raspberry Butter

SIDE ORDER

Bacon 1.15
Ham 1.15
Sausage 1.15
Hashbrown Potatoes 85

FROM THE GRIDDLE

Buttermilk Pancakes with Maple Syrup or Honey 2.50
Blueberry Pancakes 2.75
French Toast 2.20

BREAKFAST BREADS

TOAST
with butter, jams and jellies
White 90
Whole Wheat 90
Raisin 1.00
Cinnamon 90
Croissant 1.15
Danish Pastries 1.15
Fresh Rolls (2) 90
Corn or Bran Muffin 90
Toasted English Muffin 90

BEVERAGES

Melange . . . mit schlag . . . with whipped cream 80
Kapuziner—Black coffee Steamed with Milk 75
American Coffee 65
Tea 65
Hot Chocolate 65
Buttermilk 65
English Breakfast Tea 65

DAROFF DESIGN, INC./Interior Architecture and Design   MILTON GLASER/Graphic Design   THE GEORGE LANG CORP./Concept and Development

12-1-77-20 000

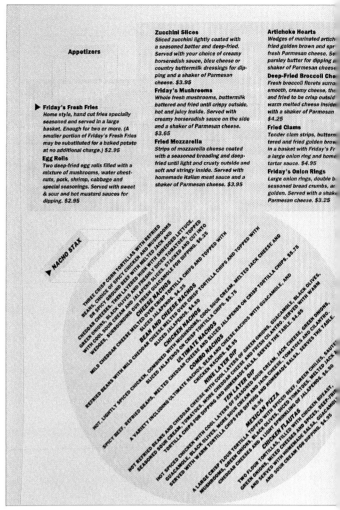

Restaurant: T.G.I. Friday's
Location: Nationwide chain headquartered in Dallas, Texas
Designer: Mike Schroeder
Illustrators: Woody Pirtle, Mike Schroeder
Specifications: Main Menu, T.G.I. Friday's
Size: 10½" x 14"
Typeface: Franklin Gothic
Paper: Kimdura
Printer: Allcraft Printing

T.G.I. Friday's 1984 main menu is in a large format and has a clean, modern look. Here, an abundance of items are presented in an organized fashion to keep from overwhelming the reader. The graphic, linear design helps focus the reader's attention. The Menu cover and interior are printed on durable Kimdura paper.

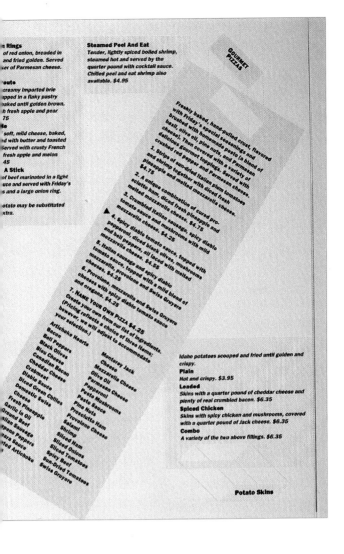

Restaurant:	T.G.I. Friday's
Location:	Nationwide chain headquartered in Dallas, Texas
Designer:	Woody Pirtle
Firm:	Pirtle Design
Illustrators:	Woody Pirtle and Gary Templin
Printer:	Allcraft Printing
Specifications:	T.G.I. Friday's Summer Fan Menu
Size:	9⅞″ x 13⅞″

On a hot summer's day, T.G.I. Friday's offers relief from the heat with this fan menu. The blade of the fan may be rotated to make the selection.

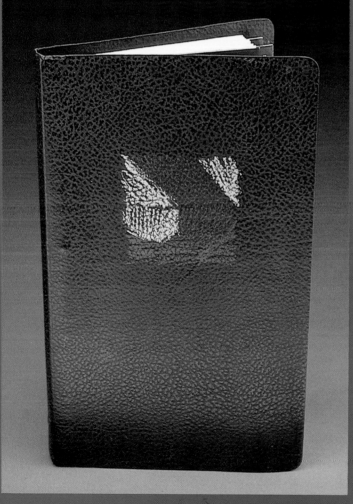

Restaurant: T.G.I. Friday's
Location: Nationwide chain headquartered in Dallas, Texas
Designer: Woody Pirtle
Firm: Pirtle Design
Illustrators: Woody Pirtle, Mark Pirtle, David Kampa, and Ken Shafer
Printer: Allcraft Printing
Specifications: T.G.I. Friday's 1983 Main Menu
Size: 7″ x 11½″
Paper: Kimdura

This spiralbound menu, the restaurant's main menu, contains well-organized indexed sections, as well as modern illustrations which head each section. This menu demonstrates how a large variety of choices can be organized so the patron can quickly zero in on what he or she wants. The food descriptions are clearly worded and well-thought-out.

Omelettes

Our omelettes are made with four eggs and are served moist unless otherwise requested. Served with hash browns and a toasted, buttered English muffin.

Three Cheese Omelette
With a mixture of green onions, sharp cheddar, Swiss, and bleu cheeses for a slightly tangy flavor. $4.75

Grand Mere Omelette
With sautéed mushrooms, crumbled bacon, melted Swiss cheese, fine herbs, and topped with mornay sauce. $5.35

Broccoli Cheese Omelette
With fresh sautéed broccoli and melted cheddar and Jack cheeses. $4.75

Spinach Omelette
With fresh sautéed spinach combined with a blend of Swiss and Jack cheeses, and mornay sauce. $4.75

Crabmeat Artichoke Omelette
With tender crabmeat and artichoke hearts sautéed in sherry and covered with mornay sauce. $5.35

Bacon and Cheddar Omelette
With crumbled bacon and cheddar cheese. $4.75

Western Omelette
With sautéed ham, onions, bell peppers, and melted cheddar cheese. $4.75

"We'll Try Anything" Omelette
Any imaginative combination of ingredients conceived by the customer. $5.35 (crabmeat and shrimp an additional $.75)

SPATS

THE ALL TIME GOOD TIME   **GOOD FOOD & DRINK PLACE**

APPETIZERS

SPEAKEASY SOUPS

Hearty homemade soup of the day. Start your meal off right, $1.95.

BIG FRENCHY'S ONION SOUP

Topped with bubbling Swiss and Parmesan Cheese, $2.55.

FRENCH FRIED ZUCCHINI

Dipped in our own batter. Super with Parmesan Cheese, $2.95.

SPATS' SHOELACES

The Seasoned French Fry, $1.95. Half Order, $1.25.

SHIRLEY'S CURLS

Bite size, hand cut, sweet red, golden fried onion rings, $2.25.

GOLLY GEE WILLIKERS! *Our onion rings are so crisp and delicious they'll curl your hair.*

FROM THE 20'S WHEN MEN WORE SPATS AND WOMEN WORE VERY LITTLE AT ALL.

Who are we? More than a Twenties style speakeasy. First and foremost we're an absolutely, positively delicious restaurant. However, our drinks are so good, so inventive, so profuse and profoundly refreshing – you may well think of us as a bar. But, whatever you choose to call us, we are indeed a special place. Because there is no place like us. Oh sure, a lot of other places sell burgers and beer, but we do not stop there. No sir, as scrumptious as they are, we have progressed well beyond burgers and beer. We're into things like crepes and casseroles and Mexican steak. Deep dish apple pie, cola cake and something wonderful called Frozen Hot Chocolate. Things no one else has – like our Secret Sauce! The stuff we put on the most mouthwatering succulent tasting, marinated hickory smoked or charbroiled barbecued chicken and ribs you have ever tasted. Ummm!

But that's not all that makes us special. In case you didn't know, we prepare every tasty morsel we serve right here in our own kitchen. With our own caring hands – even the nachos. And that goes for the steak sauce too.

No, there's no place else quite like Spats. So, whatever you're hungry for – whether you're a first timer or an old timer, welcome to the all time good time, good food and drink place. Welcome to Spats. ▲ ▲ ▲

GUACAMOLE WITH CHIPS

Muy bueno, $2.95.

GUACAMOLE & SALSA WITH CHIPS

¡Muy muy bueno! $3.95.

SALSA WITH CHIPS

¡Ole! $2.25.

CHILI CON QUESO WITH CHIPS

A Spicy Cheese Dip, $3.45.

CRISPY FRIED MUSHROOMS

With Mustard-Horseradish Sauce, $2.95.

ONION RINGS

Oversized, hand cut, golden fried rings. Exceptional, $2.25.

QUICHE APPETIZER

Delicious! Your choice, $3.35.

All items packaged to go, add 50¢.

▲▲▲

THE W. C. FIELDS. *The kind of burger that could turn its namesake from women and drink. Ahh yes!*

THE SPEEDY GONZALEZ BURGER. *Scrumptious. Tasty. Delicious. Catch this one if you can.*

Restaurant: Spats

Location: Chain restaurant headquartered in Nashville, Tennessee

Designer: Glyn Powell

Firm: Dennard Creative

Illustrators: Glyn Powell, Robin Ayres, Larry Martin, Waleo Horton, Ken Koester (all of Dennard) and Jerry Jeanmard

Printer: Jarvis Press

Specifications:

Size: 9″ x 12½″

Paper: Lustro Offset Enamel Dull White

Spats, those dandy high-buttoned shoe covers worn by men during the 1920s, is the theme of this speakeasy-style restaurant. The menu is filled with humorous illustrations and sayings designed to entertain the customers as they wait for their meals, (note the Shirley Temple in the corner with onion ring curls). Silhouettes of silent movie characters run across the top of one page, while a silhouetted minstrel singer plays in the corner. Lingo of the 1920s is used in the burger section.

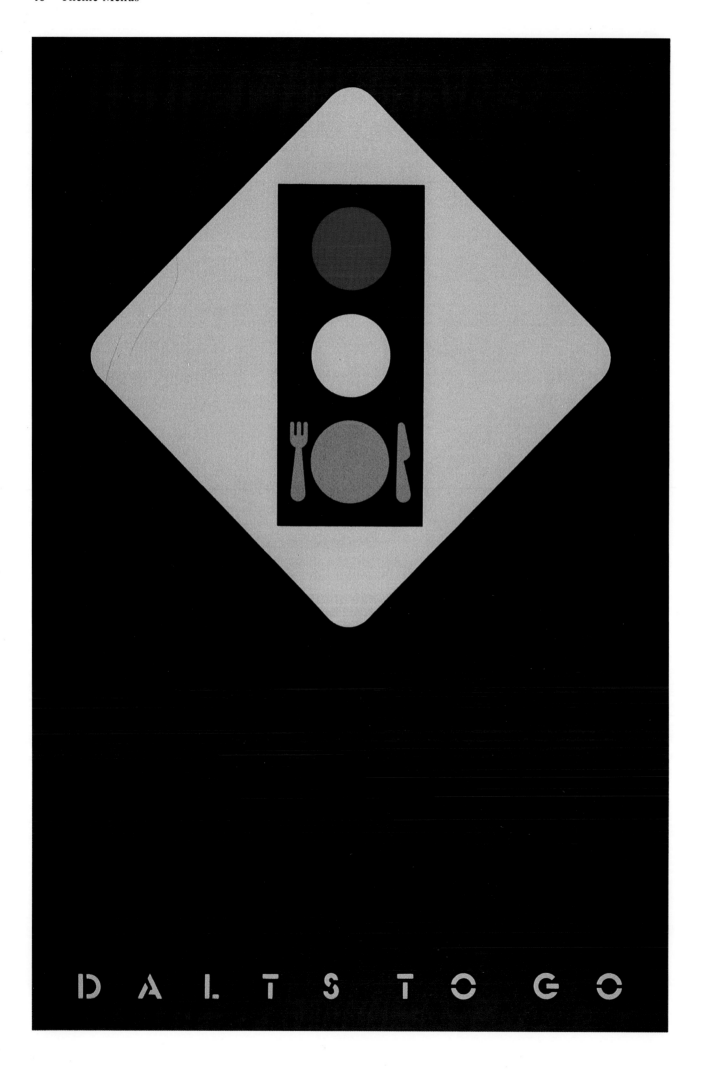

Restaurant: Dalt's
Location: Nationwide chain owned by T.G.I. Friday's, Inc., headquartered in Dallas, Texas
Designer: Woody Pirtle
Firm: Pirtle Design
Illustrator: Brian Wilburn
Copywriter: Mary Keck
Printer: Allcraft Printing
Specifications: DALT'S TO GO Menu
Size: 6″ x 9″

This carryout menu depicts a traffic light within a road sign. The designer has cleverly positioned a place setting in green by the green light, emphasizing the copy which reads "DALTS TO GO."

PHILADELPHIA STEAK SANDWICHES

Choice sirloin, thinly sliced and grilled with onions (grilled peppers also recommended) on a special Philadelphia roll.

STEAK	$3.95
CHEESE STEAK	$4.35

Above with a special cheese sauce.

PEPPERONI STEAK	$4.35

Pepperoni, mozzarella cheese and grilled onions.

SOFT TACOS

Three soft flour tortillas grilled warm.

CHILI AND CHEESE	$3.75

Filled with no bean chili, cheddar cheese, lettuce, tomatoes and onions.

CHICKEN, SOUR CREAM AND JACK CHEESE	$3.75

Filled with spicy chicken, mushrooms, sour cream, Jack cheese, lettuce, tomatoes and onions.

HAMBURGERS

Dalts Hamburgers are made from fresh U.S.D.A. choice chuck which is hand trimmed, ground and hand patted in our kitchen just before lunch and dinner. Our hamburger meat is always fresh. No fresher, juicier hamburger can be found anywhere. Grilled and served on a sesame bun and wrapped to keep the heat and juices in. Grilled onions on request.

HAMBURGER	$3.35

With mustard, lettuce, tomato, mayonnaise and pickles.

CHEESEBURGER	$3.65

With the above and 2 slices of American cheese.

BACON CHEESEBURGER	$3.75

With the above and thick sliced bacon.

CHILIBURGER	$3.75

With homemade chili, American cheese, mustard, and pickles.

MUSHROOM AND JACK BURGER	$3.95

Sauteed onions and mushrooms with Jack cheese melted on top.

MUSHROOM, BACON AND SWISS BURGER	$3.95

Sauteed mushrooms and bacon covered with melted Swiss cheese.

PATTY MELT	$3.75

A hamburger on grilled rye bread with American cheese melted on both sides.

HAMBURGER CLUB	$3.75

A Dalts cheeseburger on toasted whole wheat, double decked with bacon, lettuce, tomato and Thousand Island dressing.

DIET HAMBURGER PLATE	$3.65

A Dalts burger served side by side with cottage cheese on melon wedges and garnished with pineapple wedges.

Above with a half order of French fries 95¢ extra.

Restaurant: Dalt's

Location: Nationwide chain owned by T.G.I. Friday's, Inc., headquartered in Dallas, Texas .

Designer: Mike Schroeder

Firm: Pirtle Design

Illustrator: Mike Schroeder

Printer: Allcraft Printing

Specifications: Dalt's Summer Sun Reflector

Size: 12⅛″ x 12¼″

Paper: Mohawk Superfine

The cover's sun-bright colors reflect the hottest summer days. Even the sun sports a pair of sunglasses. But that's not all this menu reflects. Besides listing summer dishes and drinks, it doubles as a reflector, to help speed up a suntan.

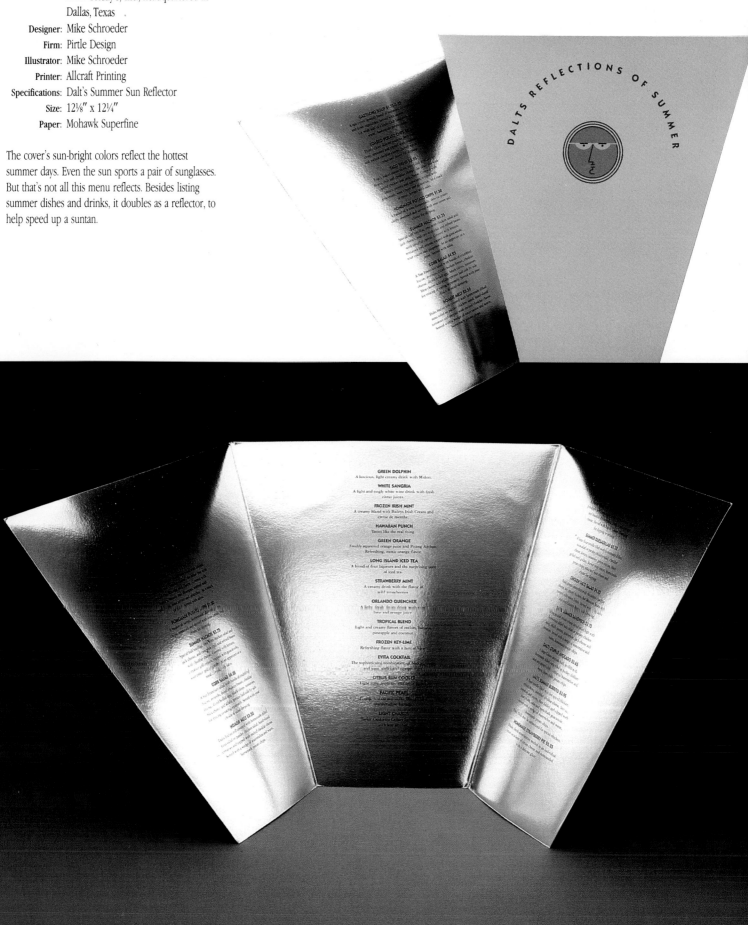

Served Every Sunday Morning and Afternoon.
Join us for Good Food and Good Times.

COFFEE CAKE / $1.25
Homemade cinnamon pecan cake. Served warm.

DALTS BELGIAN WAFFLES
Deep and tender special malt waffles.
Hot blueberries and whipped cream. $3.95
Cool, fresh strawberries (in season) and whipped cream. $4.25
Benedict with poached eggs, Canadian bacon and hollandaise sauce
and served with fruit salad. $4.25

BELGIAN STRAWBERRY SHORTWAFFLE™ / $4.25
Three Belgian waffle quarters sliced and filled with a luscious strawberry
and banana cream.

FRENCH TOAST / $3.95
Italian bread, battered and grilled. Served with bacon, sausage or ham,
hot syrup and fruit salad.

HOMEMADE PANCAKES / $3.25
Large, tender pancakes served with bacon, sausage or ham, hot syrup
and fruit salad.

DALTS EGGS / $3.75
Soft flour tortillas with mild sausage, fried eggs and melted Monterey Jack
cheese. Served with fruit salad.

EGGS BENEDICT / $4.25
Poached eggs on grilled Canadian bacon. Served on a hot biscuit
and covered with hollandaise sauce. With hash browns and fruit salad.
(Traditional Eggs Benedict with English muffin available.)

HUEVOS DALTS / $3.95
Two corn tortillas layered with ham, onions and eggs and topped with
melted colby cheese, sliced avocado and black olives. Served with refried
beans and fruit salad.

BRUNCH QUESADILLA / $4.50
A large flour tortilla filled with scrambled eggs, American cheese, green
onions, mild green chilies and bacon, then folded, grilled golden and
topped with avocado slices and sour cream. Served with salsa and fruit
salad.

BRUNCH ENCHILADAS / $4.50
Two corn tortillas filled with cheese and onions and topped with chili and
beans, eggs and melted colby cheese. Served with salsa and fruit salad.

CHICKEN, BISCUIT AND EGGS / $3.95
Poached eggs placed on an open biscuit with creamy chicken and vegetables, topped with melted cheddar cheese. Served with hash browns and
fruit salad.

JOE'S SPECIAL / $4.50
From San Francisco, a scrambled mixture of ground beef, eggs, fresh spinach,
garlic and herbs. Served with fruit salad, hash browns and a biscuit.

BRISKET AND BISCUIT / $4.25
An open biscuit topped with thick slices of tender brisket and smothered
with brisket gravy. Served with hash browns and fruit salad. (Add eggs, in
additional 50¢.)

BRISKET BEARNAISE / $4.95
An open biscuit layered with thick slices of brisket, poached eggs and
topped with bearnaise sauce. Served with hash browns and fruit salad.

BRISKET HASH / $3.95
Roasted brisket combined with onions and potatoes and sautéed until crisp.
Topped with fried eggs and served with a biscuit and fruit salad.

EGG BREAKFAST / $3.75
Three eggs with bacon, sausage or ham, hash browns and homemade
biscuit. Served with fruit salad.

OMELETTES
All omelettes served with hash browns, a homemade biscuit and fruit salad.
Benedict Omelette (With Canadian bacon and hollandaise sauce) $3.95
Spinach, Bacon and Mushroom Frittata $4.75
Denver Omelette $3.95   Mushroom and Two Cheese Omelette $3.95
Bacon and Cheese Omelette $3.95   Three Cheese Omelette $3.95
Name Your Own Omelette $4.50 (Crabmeat and shrimp an additional 50¢.)

QUICHES
A crusty shell filled with a freshly made cheese, egg and cream custard.
Served with fruit salad and dinner salad.
Seafood Quiche (With crabmeat, shrimp and Swiss cheese) $3.95
Broccoli, Zucchini, Mushroom Quiche (With fresh broccoli, zucchini,
mushrooms, Swiss and colby cheeses) $3.50

BEVERAGES
Fresh Orange Juice $.95   Tomato Juice $.95   Coffee or Hot Tea $.85
Ramos Gin Fizz   Brandy Milk Punch   Champagne

SIDE ORDERS
Toast $.50   Homemade Biscuits $.75   Hash Browns $.75
English Muffin $.50   Country or Brisket Gravy $.85

© TGI Friday's Inc. 1985 Shortwaffle is a proprietary mark of TGI Friday's Inc.
and all rights are reserved. MARFA

Restaurant: Dalt's
Location: Nationwide chain owned by
T.G.I. Friday's, Inc., headquartered
in Dallas, Texas
Designer: Mike Schroeder
Firm: Pirtle Design
Illustrator: Mike Schroeder
Printer: Allcraft Printing
Specifications: Dalt's Sunday Brunch Menu
Size: 9″ x 24⅛″
Paper: Kimdura

This two-foot-long Sunday brunch menu is
designed to accommodate the restaurant's long and
interesting list of brunch entries. The design is
itself simple and direct.

Restaurant: And That's Entertainment
Location: Montgomery, Alabama
Designer: Lew Lehrman
Firm: Design Unlimited/Culinary Concepts
Printer: Artisan Printers
Specifications:
  Size: 9″ x 12½″
  Paper: Hammermill Offset

This menu is in the form of a script on a clipboard with typewritten entries. The director's notes (comments on each of the items) are handwritten in the margins in red. The restaurant's beverage menu is featured in the Specialty chapter.

Restaurant: Dalt's
Location: Nationwide chain owned by
  T.G.I. Friday's, Inc., headquartered in
  Dallas, Texas
Designer: Woody Pirtle
Firm: Pirtle Design
Illustrator: Brian Wilburn
Printer: Allcraft Printing
Specifications: Dalt's Jukebox
  Size: 8″ x 10″

Dalt's drink menu is made special by its humor and originality. This authentic replica of a jukebox has pages that flip for food and drink selections, just as a real jukebox flips for the selection of tunes.

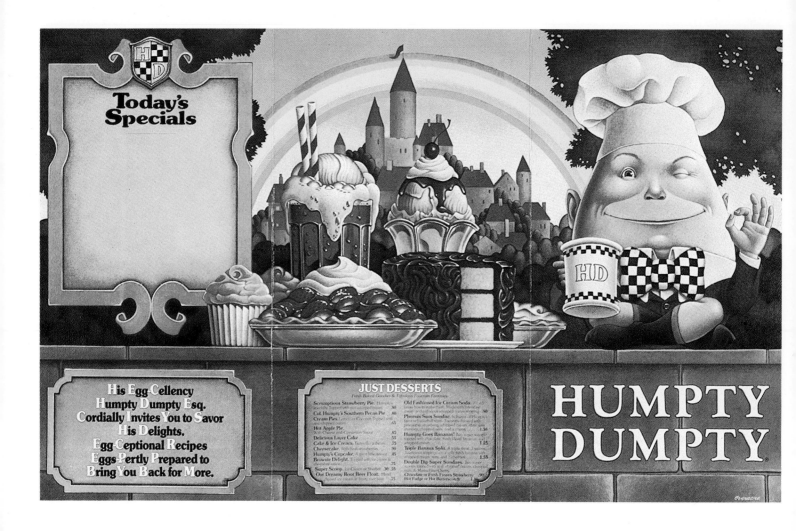

Restaurant: Humpty Dumpty
Location: Phoenix, Arizona
Designer: David Bartels
Firm: Bartels & Company
Illustrator: Gary Overacre

Humpty Dumpty is a family-oriented restaurant and coffee shop. The menu's fare has a complete array of breakfast, lunch, and dinner selections, for a light repast to a full meal. The dessert menu is on the back.

Drugstore style. Syrup and vanilla ice cream made in a soda tower for fizz and bubbles.

Chocolate
Vanilla
Cherry

Espresso is a special blend of high quality (Arabica) coffees, (grown at high altitudes), which is dark roasted, (to bring out more flavor), finely ground, (to release more flavor), and pressure brewed quickly, (to extract all the flavor without bitterness). It is truly the "heart" or "cream" of the coffee.

ESPRESSO
A demitasse of the original.

ESPRESSO ROMANO
Espresso served in the Italian manner, with a twist of lemon.

ESPRESSO CON PANNA
Espresso topped with fresh whipped cream and shaved chocolate.

CAPPUCCINO
A traditional favorite: Espresso topped with thick foamed milk.

CAFFÉ LATTE
The Italian name. (Café Au Lait in France; Cafe Con Leche in Spain)

A lighter, milkier Cappuccino: foamed milk layered with espresso and topped with a sprinkling of nutmeg.

CAFFÉ CIOCCOLOCCINO (CHOCO LA CHEEN'O)
Espresso with chocolate ice cream, topped with foamed milk and shaved chocolate.

Made thick and creamy with ice cream and old fashioned malt, if you wish.
Chocolate
Vanilla
Cherry

Restaurant:	T.G.I. Friday's
Location:	Nationwide chain headquartered in Dallas, Texas
Designer:	Woody Pirtle
Firm:	Pirtle Design
Illustrators:	Woody Pirtle, Mike Schroeder
Specifications:	Dalts Drink Menu
Size:	4⅜″ x 9¾″
Printer:	Allcraft Printing

The inside of this drink menu lists ice cream drinks and coffees. The front cover. is featured in the Specialty chapter.

2

Ethnic Dining

America is the great melting pot, and Americans are
adventurous eaters. We are fortunate to have restaurants
representing all nations of the world here in the United States.
The most popular ethnic restaurants are French, Italian,
Chinese, Japanese, Greek, Mexican, Middle Eastern, Indian,
Spanish, German, and Irish.

Because many American diners will be unfamiliar with both
the food and the language of an ethnic restaurant, it is
advantageous to explain as many food items as possible.
People love to learn. They want to know the foreign names
for different foods and methods of preparation. Generally,
diners are more adventuresome if they know exactly what is
being offered, and what the method of preparation is.

Ethnic menus seem to visually pick up on the essence of the
nation they represent, setting the stage for a foreign eating
experience. The elegant minimalist esthetics of the Japanese,
the lively gay red Chinese colors, and the rugged sagebrush of
Mexico whet the appetite for what's to come.

While there is some crossover of ethnic restaurants between
fine dining and informal dining, we've placed most of the
ethnic restaurants in this section to emphasize the variety of
flavors and colors the cuisines of the world have to offer.

Restaurant: El Torito

Location: Nationwide chain headquartered in
Irvine, California

Designer: Larry McAdams

Firm: Larry McAdams Design, Inc.

Illustrator: Larry McAdams

Specifications: Breakfast Egg Menu

Size: 13″ x 10½″ cover

Paper: Kromecoat

This well-known Mexican restaurant chain caters to a
professional clientele. The idea of a Mexican breakfast
is made more appetizing by the array of interesting
items offered. The menu, shaped like an egg, opens to
a cracked shell on one side, and a sunnyside-up egg on
the other, illustrated by the designer. Drink selections
and children's choices are included within this menu,
which is sure to add "sizzle" to any morning meal.

Restaurant: The Little Bear
Location: Bearsville, New York
Designer: Milton Glaser
Firm: Milton Glaser, Inc.
Illustrator: Milton Glaser
Specifications:
Size: 10″ x 14″ cover

Located in Bearsville, New York, two miles west of
Woodstock, The Little Bear offers cuisine from the four
main regions of China: Peking, Szechwan, Hunan, and
Canton, and includes a substantial vegetarian selection.
Open for lunch and dinner, The Little Bear serves
several unique dishes. The main dining area is an
intimate glassed-in patio overlooking the Sawkill Creek.
The menu's colors of red, yellow, and tan reflect the
restaurant's warm atmosphere, and the Chinese
characters on either side of a little bear holding a
drinking cup spell out "the little black bear." In the
winter, a "snowbear" stands at the restaurant's entrance.

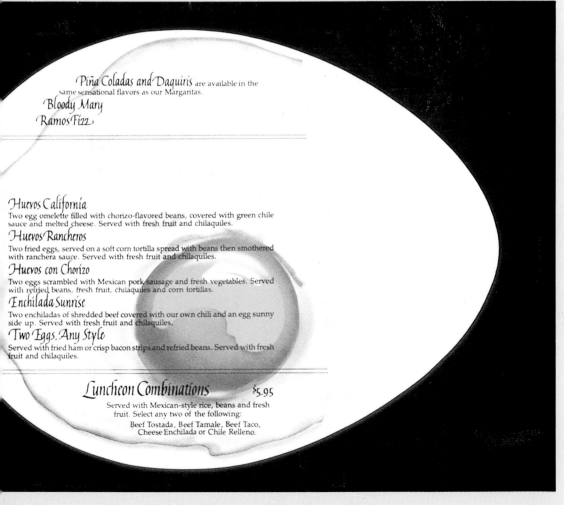

Piña Coladas and Daquiris are available in the
same sensational flavors as our Margaritas.
Bloody Mary
Ramos Fizz

Huevos California
Two egg omelette filled with chorizo-flavored beans, covered with green chile
sauce and melted cheese. Served with fresh fruit and chilaquiles.
Huevos Rancheros
Two fried eggs, served on a soft corn tortilla spread with beans then smothered
with ranchera sauce. Served with fresh fruit and chilaquiles.
Huevos con Chorizo
Two eggs scrambled with Mexican pork sausage and fresh vegetables. Served
with refried beans, fresh fruit, chilaquiles and corn tortillas.
Enchilada Sunrise
Two enchiladas of shredded beef covered with our own chili and an egg sunny
side up. Served with fresh fruit and chilaquiles.
Two Eggs, Any Style
Served with fried ham or crisp bacon strips and refried beans. Served with fresh
fruit and chilaquiles.

Luncheon Combinations $5.95
Served with Mexican-style rice, beans and fresh
fruit. Select any two of the following:
Beef Tostada, Beef Tamale, Beef Taco,
Cheese Enchilada or Chile Relleno.

Restaurant: Port of Italy
Location: Temple Hills, Maryland
Designer: Nancy Vigliatta
Firm: Design Unlimited/Culinary Concepts
Illustrator: Nancy Vigliatta
Printer: East Coast Lithographers
Die-Cutter: Freedman Cutouts
Specifications:
Size: 11″ x 11″
Paper: 12 pt. Cast coated, two sides

This menu is notable for its excellent use of die-cuts. The cover shows the lid of a die-cut spaghetti pot which, when lifted, reveals a full pot of pasta. When the page is turned, the reverse side of the pot becomes a man's head. The next page contains a napkin which, when the page is turned, becomes a sail on a sailboat. Design of a die-cut that works on both sides of a sheet displays a particularly imaginative use of form transformation.

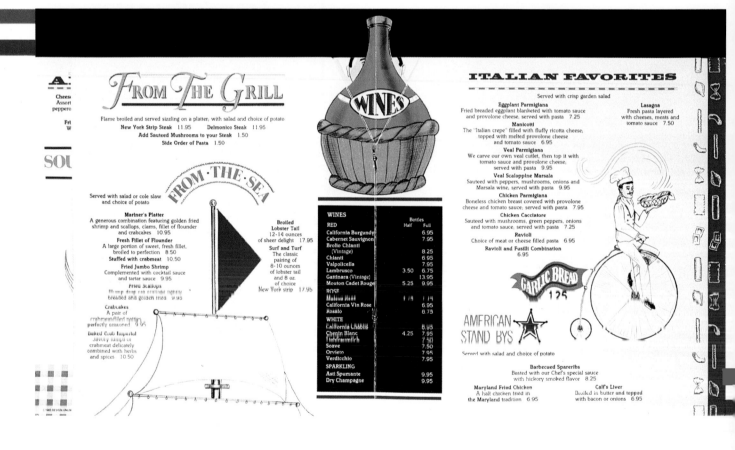

FROM THE GRILL

Flame broiled and served sizzling on a platter, with salad and choice of potato

New York Strip Steak 11.95   Delmonico Steak 11.95
Add Sauteed Mushrooms to your Steak 1.50
Side Order of Pasta 1.50

FROM THE SEA

Served with salad or cole slaw and choice of potato

Mariner's Platter
A generous combination featuring golden fried shrimp and scallops, clams, fillet of flounder and crabcakes 10.95

Fresh Fillet of Flounder
A large portion of sweet, fresh fillet, broiled to perfection 8.50
Stuffed with crabmeat 10.50

Fried Jumbo Shrimp
Complemented with cocktail sauce and tartar sauce 9.95

Fried Scallops
Plump deep sea scallops lightly breaded and golden fried 9.95

Crabcakes
A pair of crabmeat-filled patties perfectly seasoned 9.95

Baked Crab Imperial
Savory lumps of crabmeat delicately combined with herbs and spices 10.50

Broiled Lobster Tail
12-14 ounces of sheer delight 17.95

Surf and Turf
The classic pairing of 8-10 ounces of lobster tail and 8 oz. of choice New York strip 17.95

WINES

WINES	Bottles	
	Half	Full
RED		
California Burgundy		6.95
Cabernet Sauvignon		7.95
Brolio Chianti (Vintage)		8.25
Chianti		6.95
Valpolicella		7.95
Lambrusco	3.50	6.75
Gattinara (Vintage)		13.95
Mouton Cadet Rouge	5.25	9.95
ROSE		
Mateus Rosé	4.75	7.75
California Vin Rose		6.95
Rosato		8.75
WHITE		
California Chablis		8.95
Chenin Blanc	4.25	7.95
Liebfraumilch		7.50
Soave		7.50
Orvieto		7.95
Verdicchio		7.95
SPARKLING		
Asti Spumante		9.95
Dry Champagne		9.95

ITALIAN FAVORITES

Served with crisp garden salad

Eggplant Parmigiana
Fried breaded eggplant blanketed with tomato sauce and provolone cheese, served with pasta 7.25

Lasagna
Fresh pasta layered with cheeses, meats and tomato sauce 7.50

Manicotti
The "Italian crepe" filled with fluffy ricotta cheese, topped with melted provolone cheese and tomato sauce 6.95

Veal Parmigiana
We carve our own veal cutlet, then top it with tomato sauce and provolone cheese, served with pasta 9.95

Veal Scaloppine Marsala
Sauteed with peppers, mushrooms, onions and Marsala wine, served with pasta 9.95

Chicken Parmigiana
Boneless chicken breast covered with provolone cheese and tomato sauce, served with pasta 7.95

Chicken Cacciatore
Sauteed with mushrooms, green peppers, onions and tomato sauce, served with pasta 7.25

Ravioli
Choice of meat or cheese filled pasta 6.95

Ravioli and Fusilli Combination 6.95

GARLIC BREAD 1.25

AMERICAN STAND BYS

Served with salad and choice of potato

Barbecued Spareribs
Basted with our Chef's special sauce with hickory smoked flavor 8.25

Maryland Fried Chicken
A half chicken fried in the Maryland tradition 6.95

Calf's Liver
Broiled in butter and topped with bacon or onions 6.95

SANDWICHES & BURGERS

Meatball Sandwich
On Italian bread with tomato sauce
2.95
With cheese
3.25

Sausage Sandwich
own sausage on Italian bread with tomato sauce
2.95
With cheese
3.25

Reuben
ll stack of corned beef, Swiss cheese, sauerkraut
d Thousand Island dressing grilled on rye bread
3.95

Crab Cake Sandwich
perfectly seasoned crab cake on a toasted bun
3.25

Club Sandwich
A triple decker of turkey, bacon,
lettuce and tomato
2.95

Ham and Cheese
2.95
Turkey
With lettuce and tomato
2.95

Roast Beef
With lettuce and tomato
2.95
Hot Corned Beef
2.95

All burgers are served with
lettuce, tomato and French fries
Hamburger **Cheeseburger**
2.95 3.10
Bacon Cheeseburger
3.50

P·I·Z·Z·A

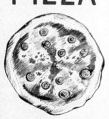

Imagine a piping hot pizza, fragrant with spices,
laden with your favorite toppings, in the perfect size
. . . and we'll create it for you!

Mushrooms	Black olives	Ground beef
Green peppers	Sausage	Bacon
Onions	Italian salami	Pepperoni

	Small	Medium	Large
Cheese	2.95	3.95	6.50
One item	3.49	4.95	7.50
Two items	3.95	5.95	8.75
Three items	4.49	6.95	9.95
Four or five items	5.25	7.95	11.25
Extra cheese	.75	1.25	1.75

Half and half pizzas are priced according to the side
with the most items.

Pizzas are available "to go".

SOLO PER BAMBINI
FOR CHILDREN ONLY

Fried Chicken
h French fries and cole slaw
3.95

Spaghetti with Tomato Sauce
1.95
With meatball
2.25

Spaghetti with Meat Sauce
2.05

GARLIC BREAD 1.00

LUNCHEON·CHOICES
SALADS

Chicken Salad Platter
Chunks of chicken, with
garnishes, on a bed of lettuce
3.50

Chef Salad
Fresh sliced meats and cheeses
atop crisp greens
3.50

Antipasto
A tempting platter of Italian salad
favorites with our own dressing
3.95

House Salad
Tossed greens and garden vegetables
1.00
Bleu cheese dressing .50 additional

ITALIAN FAVORITES

Lasagna
Fresh pasta layered with cheeses,
meats and tomato sauce
3.95

Manicotti
The "Italian crepe" filled with fluffy
ricotta cheese; topped with melted
provolone cheese and tomato sauce
3.50

Spaghetti with Meat Sauce
Our sauce is rich with ground beef
3.25

Eggplant Parmigiana
Fried breaded eggplant blanketed with meat
sauce and melted cheese; served with pasta
3.75

Chicken Parmigiana
Boneless chicken breast covered with
provolone cheese and tomato sauce;
served with pasta
3.95

Ravioli
Choice of cheese or meat filled pasta
3.50

Spaghetti with Meatballs
Our freshly made pasta with flavorful
tomato sauce and tasty meatballs
3.25

SEAFOOD

Fresh Broiled Flounder
Served with vegetable of the day
4.25

Stuffed with crabmeat
6.25

The following are served with cole slaw
and French fried potatoes

Crab Cake
3.95

Fried Shrimp Basket
3.95

Fried Clams
3.50

Fish and Chips
3.29

AMERICAN STAND BYS

Luncheon Steak
Flame broiled to your order 5.25

Calf's Liver
Broiled in butter and topped
with bacon or onions 3.75

Barbecued Spareribs
Basted with our Chef's special sauce
with hickory smoked flavor 4.25

Barbecued Beef Platter
Ground beef in a flavorful sauce on a bun;
served with French fries and cole slaw 3.95

Maryland Fried Chicken
Crisp and delicious 3.50

Homemade Chili
A cupful of our own hearty recipe 1.25

PLATA
GRANDE

Restaurant: Plata Grande
Location: Beltsville, Maryland
Designer: Kathleen Wilmes Herring
Firm: MDB Communications, Inc.
Printer: Westland Printers, Inc.
Specifications: Yellow and Black Menus
Size: yellow menu: 11½″ x 16″,
black menu: 13″ x 9¼″
Paper: Yellow Menu: Strathmore
Rhododendron, White 65/2 sheet cover;
Black Menu: Kroyden cover; Strathmore
Grandee, 80#, (ivory, gold, and
orange) inside

On the black menu, the restaurant's trademark is foil-stamped on the cover. On the yellow menu, authentic Mexican motifs are carried through the menu. These serve as educational tools telling the patrons a little about Mexican history as they wait for their orders. The restaurant's dessert menu is in the Specialty chapter.

Restaurant: Piccolo's Famous Pizza	This menu is designed as a three-dimensional stand-up
Location: Philadelphia, Pennsylvania	photograph of a pizza box, with a bubbling-hot cheesy
Designer: Lew Lehrman	pizza inside. Propped up, the pizza is at an angle to
Firm: Design Unlimited/Culinary Concepts	the table, facing the customer. The copy for the menu
Photographer: Lew Lehrman	items is in the interior of the box, behind the pizza.
Printer: East Coast Lithographers	
Die-Cutters: Freedman Cutouts	
Specifications:	
Size: 8″ x 8″	
Paper: 10 pt. Chromolux White	

Restaurant: Second Avenue Deli
Location: New York, New York
Designer: Lew Lehrman
Firm: Design Unlimited/Culinary Concepts
Printer: East Coast Lithographers
Specifications:
Size: 6¼″ x 17″
Paper: Hammermill Cover

This is the quintessential New York delicatessen with high standards to uphold. The testimonial on the front cover about the chopped liver conveys the restaurant's concern with quality. The logotype resembles Hebrew lettering, and the old photograph of a street scene on New York's Lower East Side evokes memories of how things used to be. Patrons are encouraged to take home this menu, which perfectly captures the essence of a Jewish deli.

Restaurant: Choung's
Location: Garden City, New York
Designer: Terry Choung
Cover Art: Handmade satin and silk dolls from Hong Kong
Specifications:
Size 9¼″ x 14″

The owner of Choung's, who designed the menu, first came upon the concept at the Peninsula Hotel in Hong Kong. After simplifying the original *idea*, he purchased a number of handmade silk and satin figurines from an arts and crafts center in Hong Kong. Each figurine represents a character from Chinese mythology, and has a richly symbolic story behind it. The menus are covered with protective plastic and lined with black velvet. The owner comments that customers love the menus so much, they try to walk away with them.

Restaurant: Primera
Location: Houston, Texas
Designer: Robin Smith
Firm: Design Unlimited/Culinary Concepts
Printer: East Coast Lithographers
Specifications:
Size: 8½″ x 7¾″
Paper: 12 pt. Coated, two sides, laminated

Primera is a hotel restaurant with flair. Featuring freshly made pasta, the menu conveys freshness through the use of white space. The pasta box in the colors of the Italian flag is used on the logo. This restaurant, in the Sheraton Crown Hotel, is owned by Servico, Inc.

Restaurant:	Papa's
Location:	Storrs, Connecticut
Designer:	Monica Heymann
Firm:	MGH Studio
Printer:	Triad Press
Specifications:	
Size:	11″ x 9″
Paper:	Leatherbound cover; Filare Album Press inside; Quintessence 80# gloss menu inserts

The motif of this small, family-style Italian restaurant is based on a real family photo album. The menu features each member of the Testa family, which owns and operates Papa's. Each food section features photos of family members at different stages in their lives, with short anecdotes in handwritten captions. On the leatherbound cover is a photo of the Testa family.

Gulf
of
Mexico

N
W • E
S

CAFÉ OLÉ
RESTAURANT & CANTINA

COMBINATIONS

Served with Mexican-style rice and re

No. 1	Enchilada		No. 5
No. 2	Taco	$3.50	No. 6
No. 3	Chile Relleno		No. 7
No. 4	Tamale		No. 8
			No. 9
			No. 10
			No. 1

BURRITOS

Burrito Especial
Soft flour tortilla filled with shredded beef, beans and cheese
Topped with ranchero sauce. Sour cream garnish.

Burrito Verde
Lean diced pork, simmered in green chile sauce, and refried
wrapped in a flour tortilla. Sour cream garnish.

Burrito de Pollo
Tender pieces of chicken, refried beans and cheese rolled int
and covered with enchilada sauce

Burrito Colorado
Cubed beef, cooked in red sauce with beans, rolled in a flou

ENCHILADAS

Enchiladas Carnes
Tender pieces of beef, blended with a spicy spanish sauce, fo
corn tortillas. Topped with more sauce and a combination of
Complemented with refried beans and sour cream.

Enchiladas Rancheras
Corn tortillas rolled and stuffed with cheese, smothered with
Served with Mexican-style rice and refried beans. Guacamol
cream.

Restaurant: Café Olé Restaurant and Cantina
Location: Boise, Idaho
Designer: Dennis Chase
Illustrator: Dennis Chase
Specifications:
Size: 16″ x 12½″

Against the background of an antique treasure map, complete with a directional indicator and a Mexican coastline, is a hot desert scene in intense reds and oranges that would whet anyone's appetite for a Mexican meal. The gridwork and coastline from the front cover are carried as a design element through the inside pages of the menu. A special child's plate is included in the main menu. The menu was designed to match the restaurant's decor of Mexican tile, mahogany tables, and plants.

...lada
...adas $4⁹⁵
...relleno

...ile relleno
...chile relleno
...tamale

...lf
...f
...ico

$3⁹⁵

$3⁶⁵

$3⁴⁵

$3⁶⁵

Mexico

$4²⁵

$4⁰⁰

COMBINATIONS OLÉ

Served with Mexican-style rice and refried beans.

No. 12   Taco, enchilada, chile relleno
No. 13   Taco, chile relleno, tostada $6²⁵
No. 14   Enchilada, tostada, tamale

CHILD'S PLATE

For children under 12 years of age. $2⁷⁵

Choice of one:
Taco, tamale, enchilada, or small bean and cheese burrito. Served with Mexican-style rice and refried beans.

Enchiladas Suizas $4⁰⁰
Two tortillas dipped in tomatillo green sauce, stuffed with chunks of chicken. Rolled and topped with more sauce and melted cheese. Served with Mexican-style rice and refried beans. Sour cream garnish.

Carnitas Enchiladas $4²⁵
Tender pieces of pork, blended with a spicy spanish sauce, folded into two corn tortillas. Topped with more sauce and a combination of melted cheeses. Complemented with refried beans and sour cream.

FAVORITOS

Tostada $3²⁵
Crisp flour tortilla shell covered with refried beans, shredded beef or chicken and cut lettuce. Guacamole and sour cream garnish.

Taquitos (5) $3⁹⁰
Crisp corn tortillas filled and stuffed with shredded seasoned beef. Served with Mexican-style rice and refried beans. Sour cream and guacamole garnish.

Flautas $3⁶⁵
Two crisp flour tortillas filled with seasoned beef, on a bed of shredded lettuce with avocado sauce, sour cream and fresh tomato. Served with Mexican-style rice and refried beans.

Hamburger $2⁵⁰
Beef patty served open face on a toasted bun. Garnished with onion, tomato slice and guacamole. Cheese 25¢ extra.

Restaurant: Caliente Cab Company
Location: New York, New York
Designer: Jane Barbara
Firm: Menu Makers Plus
Illustrator: Jane Barbara
Printer: Menu Makers Plus
Specifications:
Size: 10″ x 8″

This Greenwich Village Mexican cafe is a lively and casual spot. The clientele includes students from nearby New York University and other schools, young professionals, and local tourists. The restaurant provides music from a jukebox. In the front window, an old Studebaker car is disguised as a cab. A caricature of the imposter cab appears on the menu cover, mounted on a lift that resembles a cactus.

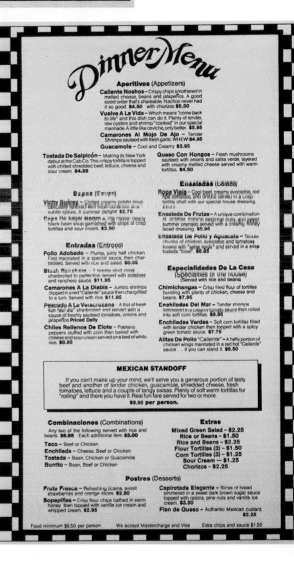

3

Fine Dining

Usually associated with formality, fine dining embodies the essence of the good life. These restaurants graciously serve their customers in establishments with tablecloths, waiters, and an atmosphere suitable for heads of state or royalty. The atmosphere is amiable, and manners are observed.

Fine dining establishments often have oversized menus, and a limited menu selection as their emphasis is more on atmosphere and quality than on variety.

Here are some menus from fine dining establishments around the country. Each restaurant seems to emphasize what they do best through their menus. For example, Lutèce's menu displays the many medals and awards that the chef, André Soltner has received. The artist Redoute's roses on the front cover symbolize the perfection sought by the restaurant.

Fine dining restaurants are generally open only for lunch and dinner, and the prices are usually high. The menus tend to be fairly classical, but within these boundaries, there is plenty of room for creativity.

MENU I	May 8-12 June 5-9 July 3-7	July 31-August 4 August 28-September 1 September 25-29 October 23-27
MENU II	May 15-19 June 12-16 July 10-14	August 7-11 September 4-8 October 2-6 October 30-November 3
MENU III	May 22-26 June 19-23 July 17-21	August 14-18 September 11-15 October 9-13 November 6-10
MENU IV	May 29-June 2 June 26-30 July 24-28	August 21-25 September 18-22 October 16-20 November 13-17

THE WINE CELLAR

Restaurant: The Wine Cellar

Location: Newporter Resort, Newport Beach, California

Designer: Steven Uyehara

Firm: Matrix Design

Illustrator: Gene Summers

Printer: Colorwest Graphics

Specifications:

Size: 9″ x 12″

Paper: 88# Strathmore writing cover, Bristol laid finish interior

The Wine Cellar is an intimate and exclusive dining retreat at the Newporter Resort, seating a maximum of 32 people at a time. The restaurant's menu works on a rotating basis, changed each week; there are four menus in all, offering classic French cuisine to an affluent clientele with discriminating tastes. The watercolor illustrations are by the resort's owner.

Restaurant: Crystal Pavilion
Location: Kansas City, Missouri
Designer: Milton Glaser
Firm: Milton Glaser, Inc.
Printer: Hallmark, Inc.
Specifications: Dinner Menu and Dessert and Wine List
Size: 10" x 15" dinner cover;
5" x 15" dessert and wine list
Paper: Mohawk Superfine 120# Bristol

Conceived by Joseph Baum and designed by Phil George, the Crystal Pavilion serves as the centerpiece of the Heartland Market, which is essentially a mall comprising several food and spirits retail establishments as well as several eateries ranging from a full-service deli to self-service fast food outlets. The Crystal Pavilion evokes a sense of luxury, outstanding service, and excellent cuisine. Its clientele includes expense-account businesspeople, social organization luncheon groups, tourists, and well-heeled locals. The menus reflect the color scheme of the interior, also developed by Milton Glaser, Inc., to express a sense of light and cheerfulness.

Restaurant: Richard Perry
Location: St. Louis, Missouri
Designer: Richard Perry
Illustrator: James Riddle
Printer: Cliff Kelly, Inc.
Specifications:
Size: 8¾″ x 8¾″ cover
Paper: Strathmore Beau Brilliant

The unique feature of this menu is its adaptability. Designed by the restaurant's owner, the menu's outer cover is a rich stock with an embossed logo of the restaurant's name. In the center, an embossed ruled box frames an illustration by James Riddle, which is attached separately to the cover. The interior of the menu features two pockets into which daily food listings, handwritten by the owner, can be inserted, making it possible to use the same cover for lunch, brunch, or dinner—a very cost-effective solution.

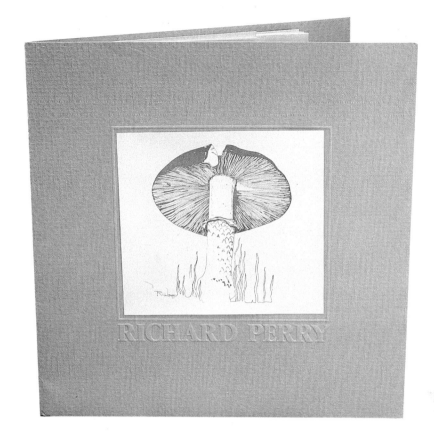

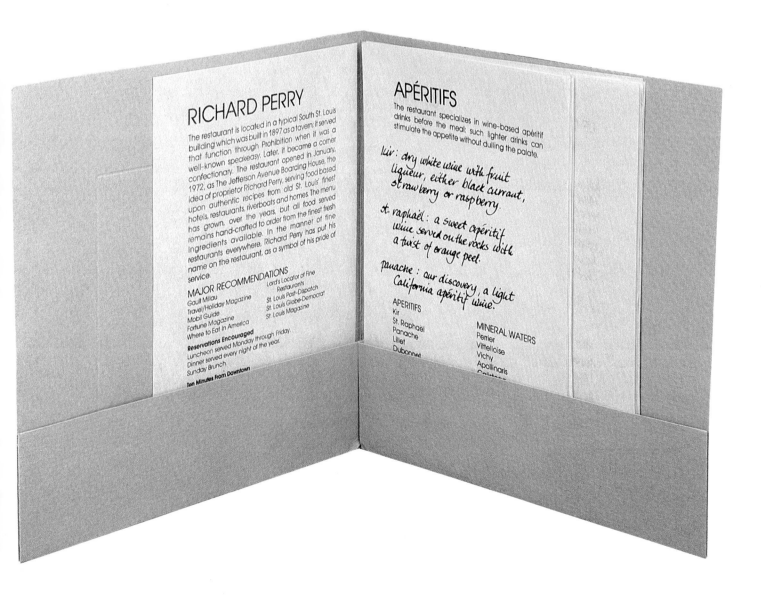

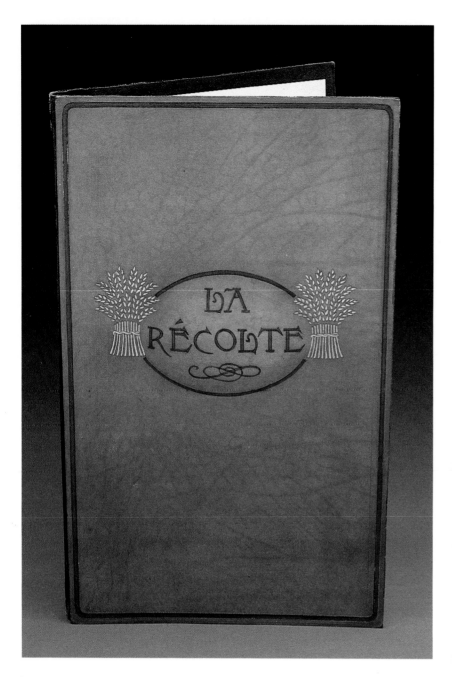

Restaurant: La Récolte
Location: New York, New York
Designer: Charles R. Alvey
Firm: Intercontinental Hotels Corp
Printer: Optima Press
Specifications:
Size: 8½″ x 14¼″
Paper: Parchtone (French) 65# cover

La Récolte is the result of a dream of a team of
internationally trained chefs and food and beverage
experts.

The name La Récolte was chosen to reflect the idea
of a bountiful harvest of the finest foods, symbolized in
the logo by two golden sheaves of wheat. The
embossed leather menu covers are handmade and are
imported from Hungary.

The menu selections are seasonal, and depend on
what's available daily in the market, and fresh foods are
imported weekly from France.

Restaurant: Harvest
Location: Cambridge, Massachusetts
Designer: Milton Glaser
Firm: Milton Glaser, Inc.
Illustrator: Milton Glaser
Printer: Blum Associates
Specifications:
Size: 15¾" x 11"
Paper: Mohawk Superfine, Eggshell White

This menu is in a poster format, dated and printed with the daily specials. Between the lettering, the artist has cleverly incorporated the moon motif, showing it in its different phases.

APPETIZERS

TIMBALE OF SMOKED TROUT	7.75
with Caviar & Julienne Vegetable Beurre Blanc	
CORIANDER GRAVLAX	6.50
with Watercress-Lemon Mayonnaise	
COUNTRY GOOSE TERRINE	5.00
with Prosciutto & Raisins	
SAUTEED LOBSTER IN PASTRY	6.50
with Julienne Leeks & Herbs	
MOUSSELINE OF FIVE VEGETABLES	6.50
with their Salads & Red Pepper Coulis	
CHILLED OYSTERS ON THE HALF SHELL	6.00
with Broccoli & Asparagus Tips & Tomato Vinaigrette	
STRUDEL OF WILD MUSHROOMS	6.50

MAIN COURSES

GRILLED FILET OF BEEF	19.00
with Brunoise of Vegetables & Roquefort Butter	
BROILED NORWEGIAN SALMON	19.50
with Crayfish, Caviar & Lobster Sauce	
SAUTEED KOSHER CHICKEN	16.00
with Sun Dried Tomatoes, Wild Mushrooms, Garlic, Capers & Fresh Pasta	
STUFFED NOISETTES OF LAMB	18.00
with Tomato Vinaigrette, Lemon & Asparagus	
SAUTEED BREAST OF GOOSE	18.00
with Juniper Berries, Gin, & Foie Gras	
SAUTEED DOVER SOLE	19.50
with Boissiere	
SAUTEED SWEETBREADS	17.50
with Spinach, Leeks, Smithfield Ham & Pleurottes	

SALADS

SALAD OF BUFFOLA MOZZARELLA	4.75
with Mixed Greens, Asparagus, Cherry Tomatoes, & Virgin Olive Oil	
SALAD OF MIXED GREENS	5.00
with Endive, Fiddleheads, Oranges, Grapes, Mixed Nuts & Sherry Vinaigrette	
HARVEST SALAD	1.75

AFTER DINNER

| SELECTION OF ASSORTED CHEESES | 3.75 |

PLEASE, PIPES & CIGARS IN THE CAFE ONLY

Restaurant:	C.J. Fish & Company
Location:	Peter's Landing, Huntington Harbor, California
Art Director:	Deborah Sussman
Designer:	Nancy Zaslavsky
Firm:	Sussman/Prejza & Company
Printer:	LithoGraphix
Specifications:	
Size:	6½″ x 12½″ cover
Paper:	Quintessence

This appealing menu succeeds brilliantly in preparing a diner for the coming meal at this waterfront summerhouse fish restaurant. Tastefully executed, the menu suggests a sensual consciousness. The cream-colored daily bulletin with pastel-colored fish and lobsters on the blackboard reinforces the sensual style. The daily bulletin folds up as a mailer, and is sealed with a gold fish stamp.

Restaurant: The Terrace Restaurant
Location: Kennett Square, Pennsylvania
Designer: Niki Bonnett
Firm: Niki Bonnett Design
Printer: DLG Business Group
Specifications:
Size: 8″ x 15½″ cover
Paper: 10 pt. Carolina Cover stock cover; 65# Curtin Linen Eggshell inserts

For the menu cover of this restaurant located in Longwood Gardens, an immense botanical garden in the Pennsylvania countryside, the client requested a floral theme. The artist located a 19th-century Amish quilt, details of which are used on the covers, which are changed seasonally (this cover is for the spring/summer menu). The inside of the cover shows a photo of the entire quilt, accompanied by a brief history telling how each block of the quilt was created by a different woman, and then stitched together at a quilting bee.

The food listing itself is an insert, decorated with clip art, which can be easily changed for dinner, lunch, or holidays. The restaurant is part of the Restaurant Associates group.

Restaurant: The Sea Grill
Location: New York, New York
Designer: Chermayeff & Geismar
Printer: DLG Business Group
Specifications:
Size: 8¼″ x 14″ cover
Paper: Tweedweave Cover White 80#,
Vicksburg Starwhite

The Sea Grill, a New York City establishment in Rockefeller Center which features a large selection of fresh fish grilled over hardwood coals and grapevines, presents a menu that equals the appeal of its offerings. The elegant, all-white cover is embossed with a variety of fish and shellfish, and is gold-foil stamped with the restaurant's logo. The inside flap of the menu lists the names of all the fish shown on the cover. The Sea Grill is part of the Restaurant Associates group.

Restaurant:	Towne Club
Location:	Dallas, Texas
Designers:	Lowell Williams and Bill Carson
Firm:	Lowell Williams Design, Inc.
Printer:	Heritage Press
Specifications:	Dinner Menu and Wine List
Size:	8½″ x 14″ menu;
	10″ x 6½″ wine list
Paper:	Fabriano Murillo #501

Towne Club is a private dining club for young professionals. Marbled paper frames the restaurant's logo, mounted on the front of the menu. The companion wine list, which is smaller and has a hard cover made of burgundy fabric, compliments the dinner menu. The look conveys classic elegance.

Restaurant: The Bear Cafe
Location: Bearsville, New York
Designer: Milton Glaser
Firm: Milton Glaser, Inc.
Illustrator: Milton Glaser

Specifications:

Size: 7⅜″ x 14¼″ cover

The Bear Cafe features continental cuisine. Originally opened in a renovated barn in 1972, the Cafe was remodeled in 1981. It now has a main dining room and bar that are cantilevered over the Sawkill Creek, with floor-to-ceiling windows overlooking the creek and the surrounding Catskill Mountains. In warm weather, streamside dining is available on the bluestone terrace. The bear silhouetted against a full moon on the menu cover is an appropriate symbol for this country setting, and the menu's black, brown, and orange color scheme compliments the rustic, yet contemporary, decor of the restaurant's interior.

The Bear Cafe, winner of a Silver Spoon Award in 1984, is open six days a week for breakfast, lunch, and dinner. Specialities of the house include *sincrinozatas*, Norweigan salmon, and pasta with smoked trout.

Restaurant: Sinclair's
Location: Lake Forest, Illinois
Designer: David Bartels
Firm: Bartels & Company
Illustrator: Gregg MacNair
Printer: Art Craft Lithographers
Specifications:
Size: 6½″ x 11″ cover
Paper: 100# Kromecoat

Sinclair's (owned by the proprietor of Gordon) has a menu which features American cuisine and serves an upscale suburban clientele. The menu, which has won numerous design awards, contains hand-lettered entries. Its companion wine list is featured in the Specialty chapter.

Restaurant: Lutèce
Location: New York, New York
Designer: André Soltner
Illustrator: Pierre-Joseph Redouté
Specifications:
Size: 11″ x 14″

Lutèce's menu, designed by its proprietor-chef, totally conveys the restaurant's essence: the presentation of food at its finest. The beautiful and elegant roses on the front cover, painted by the 19th-century French artist Redouté (known as the "Raphael of the roses"), symbolize perfection. On the inside cover, Soltner has chosen to display his well-deserved medals and awards for distinguished practice of culinary artistry.

Restaurant:	Windows on the World
Location:	New York, New York
Designer:	Milton Glaser
Firm:	Milton Glaser, Inc.
Illustrator:	Milton Glaser
Specifications:	Wine List
Size:	$6\frac{1}{2}''$ x $14\frac{3}{4}''$

Located atop Manhattan's famous World Trade Center, Windows on the World is just that. The restaurant is surrounded by windows and diners can see a panoramic view of New York while enjoying their meal or relaxing with coctails.

Restaurant: Quinn's Fish Market
Location: Seattle, Washington
Designer: Paula Cox
Firm: Martin & Cox
Illustrator: Paul Huber
Calligrapher: Carolyn Brooks
Printer: Heath Printers
Specifications: Dinner Menu
Size: 7″ x 12″ cover
Paper: Starwhite Vicksburg

The menu's cover illustration shows the view from the window of the restaurant, which is located at Shilshole Bay Marina in Seattle. The restaurant serves seafood and barbecued foods and is known in Seattle for having one of the largest salad bars featuring almost 100 items. There are separate menus for hors d'oeuvres, lunch, and dinner.

With your luncheon enjoy our complimentary
piping hot toasted beer cheese croutons.

PPETIZERS

Fried Potato Skins
Fried golden brown topped with cheddar cheese and
crumbled bacon and served with our delicious sour cream
dip. $3.95

Fried Zucchini
Fresh large slices fried in our own Italian style
breadcrumbs to a golden brown with cheese sauce for
dipping. $2.95

Fried Gruyere Cheese
Imported from Switzerland and cut into sticks breaded
lightly with herbs and fried golden, served with a zesty
Marinara sauce. $4.95

Skins and Zucchini Combo
Two of our favorite appetizers. Fried potato skins topped
with cheese and bacon and jumbo slices of fried zucchini.
$3.95

Fried Calamari
Tender calamari fried golden brown and accompanied by
marinara sauce for dipping. $4.95

SEAFOOD BAR

Jumbo Shrimp Cocktail
Extra large, tender shrimp highlighted with our tangy
cocktail sauce. $5.50

Maryland Crabmeat Cocktail
Fresh jumbo lumps of prized blue crab accented with our
tangy cocktail sauce.$5.95

Clams on the Half Shell
Fresh clams from the icy North Atlantic, served with
tangy cocktail sauce and grated horseradish. $3.95

Oysters on the Half Shell
Fresh plump Eastern oysters served with our tangy
cocktail sauce and grated horseradish. Your server will
notify you when Chincoteaques are available. $4.95

Clams and Oysters on the Half Shell
A fresh combination from our Raw Bar, accompanied by
a tangy cocktail sauce, grated horseradish and lemon.
$4.95

OUPS

French Onion Soup Gratinee
Fresh naturally sweet onions, sauteed until golden brown
then married with dry sherry and a robust beef broth,
baked under a crust of Gruyere cheese. $2.50

Seafood Gumbo Creole
Our version of a New Orleans Classic, shrimp, scallops
and crabmeat simmered with tomato, pepper, okra,
onions, garlic, along with gumbo file. $2.75

Chef's Soup of the Day
Your server will quote our chef's freshly made offering of
the day. $1.95

ASTA

Fettuccine with Four Cheeses
Freshly cooked spinach pasta blended in a creamy butter
sauce and topped with herb, fontina, parmesan and bleu
cheeses for a unique flavor experience. $5.95

Fettuccine Neptune
Shrimp, scallops and crabmeat lightly sauteed and
blended in a light cream sauce with parmesan cheese over
freshly cooked spinach pasta. $6.95

Seafood Stuffed Pasta Shells
Jumbo pasta shells stuffed with a mixture of shrimp,
crabmeat, scallops, creamy ricotta cheese and chopped
spinach, baked in a zesty Marinara sauce and topped
with freshly grated cheese. $6.95

HITES

Domestics, White

101 **Chardonnay, Parducci**
Full bodied with a touch of oak in the taste and
bouquet. $13.95

102 **Chardonnay, Raymond**
Beautiful balance of fruit and moderate oak dry
finish. $22.95

103 **Chardonnay, San Martin**
Rich, medium dry with a pronounced finish.
$12.95

104 **Fume Blanc, Beringer**
Herbal aroma, soft oak dry finish. $12.95

105 **Sauvignon Blanc, Parducci**
A bold, rich fruity nose, with a soft, dry finish.
$11.95

106 **Chenin Blanc, Dry, Callaway**
Delicate refreshing aroma, with complex fruity
characters. $14.95

107 **Chenin Blanc, Fetzer**
Crisp, light, delicate fruity flavors. $10.95

108 **Pinot Noir Blanc, Sebastiani**
Dry crisp and light, delicate fruity flavors, blush
color. $10.95

109 **Johannisberg Riesling,
Chateau St. Michelle**
Delicate honeysuckle fragrance with dry honey
and fruit finish. $11.95

Imports, White

110 **Pouilly Fuisse, St. Aubin**
A fruity well balanced white burgundy with a dry
crisp finish. $19.95

111 **Soave, Bolla**
Rich, medium dry with a pronounced subtle finish.
$8.95

112 **Liebfraumilch, Blue Nun**
A rich, spicy aroma, flower like finish. $9.95

ROSÉ

201 **Lancers**
Full of fruit, refreshing and slightly sweet. $8.95

REDS

301 **Gamay Beaujolais, Beaulieu**
Displays deep color and a lovely fruit bouquet.
$9.95

302 **Pinot Noir, Robert Mondavi**
Smooth, complex and hearty. Reminiscent of a great
French burgundy. $15.95

303 **Cabernet Sauvignon, Carneros Creek**
A bold, berry like aroma. A robust varietal.
$22.95

304 **Cabernet Sauvignon, Paul Masson**
A delicate, rich, fruity dry finish. $10.95

305 **Cabernet Sauvignon, Robert Mondavi**
Rich, full bodied, intense, velvety characteristics.
$21.95

306 **Zinfandel, Sutter Home**
Full bodied, with raspberry like aroma. $12.95

310 **Beaujolais Villages, Drouhin**
Delicate, light and fruity. $12.95

311 **St. Emillion, Chateau Laroque**
Well balanced, medium body with an elegant
finish. $14.95

HAMPAGNES

401 **Hanns Kornell Brut**
From Napa Valley, soft and fruity with a dry
finish. $17.95

402 **Mumms Cordon Rouge**
Dry intense flavor, with a natural fruit bouquet.
$29.95

403 **Dom Perignon**
World famous, dry and elegant. $75.00

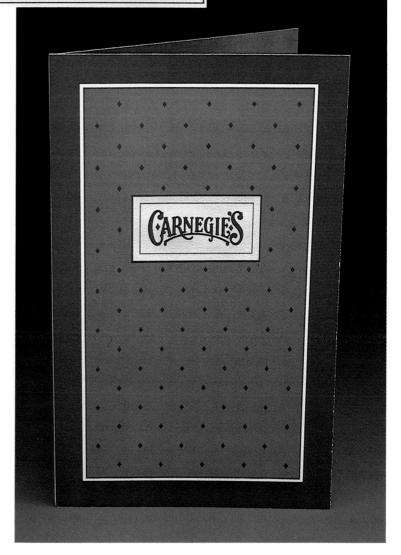

Restaurant: Carnegie's

Location: East Coast chain owned by Marriott/Host

Designers: Phil Buck and Larry McAdams

Printer: Kenyon Press

Specifications:

Size: 9½" x 15" cover;
28½" x 15" full open spread

Paper: Hopper Chambray

This menu conveys high-ticket elegant dining. The
placement of food items is a good example of savvy
merchandising. The menu first opens to the appetizer
and wine selections. The right panel opens further to
dinner and dessert selections. Strategic placement of
the wine list next to the appetizers results in more
frequent appetizer orders. Inclusion of the wine list
lowered the unit price of menus by half.

Restaurant:	Gordon
Location:	Chicago, Illinois
Designer:	David Bartels
Firm:	Bartels & Company
Illustrator:	Alain Gauthier
Printer:	Art Craft Lithographers
Specifications:	
Size:	6½″ x 11″ cover
Paper:	100# Kromecoat

Gordon is a continental-style restaurant in Chicago, catering mostly to business people. The menu design, which has won numerous awards, is an example of David Bartel's playful philosophy of menu design: the menu is a vehicle for starting a conversation, thereby relaxing the customers and setting the tone for an enjoyable meal. (Gordon's wine menu is featured in the Specialty chapter.)

4
American Regional Menus

Americans once thought that France had the only cuisine that
had earned the right to be referred to as regional. But it has
become evident that America's "provinces," or subregions, are
just as varied as those of France. The biggest news in food
over the past few years has been the recognition and
promotion of America's regional cuisines. New Orleans has
perhaps the most widely appreciated regional cooking,
however, Western barbecue, "California Cuisine," Tex-Mex,
Mexican, Southern cooking, and Northeastern seafood and
chowders are becoming known around the world.

The American Harvest Restaurant

Restaurant: The American Harvest Restaurant
Location: New York, New York
Designer: Hilton International in-house design staff
Photographer: William Margerian
Printer: Panorama Press
Specifications:
Size: 15″ x 11″
Paper: 100# Husky Hibulk

The objective of this restaurant is to present the freshest foods, at their peak of flavor, prepared in regional American cuisine. The menu covers emphasize a fresh, bountiful harvest, using the still-life photography of William Margerian. Each month, the covers and the menus change to showcase foods at the peak of the harvest and the restaurant's regional food festivals. This restaurant is operated by Hilton International and located in the Vista Hotel in lower Manhattan. The restaurant's interior displays American antiques, and features a giant photomural at the entrance which further dramatize the current harvest.

An Unexpected Shower of Tortellini in the Piazza Nettuno in Bologna.

Restaurant: The Four Seasons
Location: New York, New York
Designer: Milton Glaser
Firm: Milton Glaser Inc.
Illustrator: Milton Glaser
Printer: Panorama Press
Specifications:
Size: 7″ x 11″
Paper: Bold Brilliant Cover, 80# text

Milton Glaser adds a bit of his characteristic humor to this otherwise classical art. Featuring Bolognese cuisine, the menu cover, entitled "an unexpected shower of Tortellini in the Piazza Nettuno in Bologna," needs no further explanation. The tortellini motif appears again as a border around the inside of the cover, and is a divider between menu entries. The menu was designed for a one-time event celebrating Bolognese cuisine at The Four Seasons.

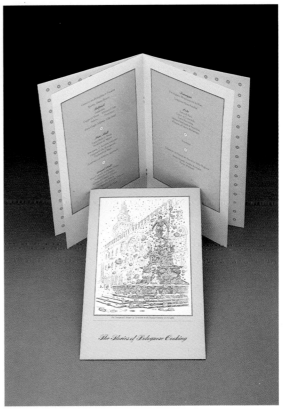

Restaurant: American Restaurant
Location: Kansas City, Missouri
Designer: Milton Glaser
Firm: Milton Glaser, Inc.
Illustrator: John James Audubon
Printer: Vile-Goller Fine Art and Lithography
Specifications:
    Size: 10½″ x 16″
    Paper: Kromecoat, 10 pt. stock

American regional cuisine is featured at this restaurant. The cover print of a wild turkey, the most traditional of American birds, is from the collection of the National Audubon Society Library collection. The original was painted in 1825 at the Beech Woods Plantation in West Feliciana Parish, Louisiana. White stars on the inside silver cover are picked up from the star on the logo. The stars and stripes on the logo give the menu a contemporary accent, while still holding elements of the Americana theme.

Restaurant:	American Festival Cafe
Location:	New York, New York
Designer:	Tom Geismar
Firm:	Chermayeff & Geismar Associates
Printer:	DLG Business Group
Specifications:	
Size:	8¼″ x 14″
Paper:	Champion Kromecoat

The restaurant is an exuberant celebration of Americana. The floors are tiled in the patterns and colors of early American patchwork quilts, and the traditional Amish "basket-of-fruit" pattern is repeated on the menu cover. A changing display of primitive folk art, loaned by the Museum of American Folk Art, is housed in glass cases between dining room alcoves. The menu changes frequently following seasonal harvests. The restaurant serves breakfast, lunch, brunch, supper, and dinner, and also celebrates seasonal festivals. It is part of the Restaurant Associates group.

Restaurant: Hanover's
Location: New Jersey
Designer: Lew Lehrman
Firm: Design Unlimited/Culinary Concepts
Illustrator: Lew Lehrman
Specifications:
Size: 9½″ x 15″

Hanover's specializes in regional American cuisine. The painting on the cover is warm and inviting, reminiscent of an Americana knicknack collection. The menu inside is detailed with descriptions of the different regional cuisines. Hanover's is owned by the Campbell Soup Company.

Restaurant: Massachusetts Bay Company
Location: Boston, Massachusetts
Designer: Sam Szoka
Firm: Business Image, Inc.
Printer: Business Image, Inc.
Specifications:
Size: 8″ x 11″
Paper: Strathmore Rhododendron 2/sheet

Local patrons, hotel guests, and tourists enjoy the unique seafood preparation and upscale dining experience of the Massachusetts Bay Company. A traditional New England seafood house, the decor consists of a brass cafe ceiling, bare wood tables, and photographic wall murals of waterfront scenes.

Restaurant: The American Harvest Restaurant

Location: New York, New York

Designer: Hilton International in-house
design staff

Photographer: William Margerian

Printer: Panorama Press

Specifications:

Size: 15″ x 11″

Paper: 100# Husky Hibulk

The objective of this restaurant is to present the freshest foods, at their peak of flavor, prepared in regional American cuisine. The menu covers emphasize a fresh, bountiful harvest, using the still-life photography of William Margerian. Each month, the covers and the menus change to showcase foods at the peak of the harvest and the restaurant's regional food festivals. This restaurant is operated by Hilton International and located in the Vista Hotel in lower Manhattan. The restaurant's interior displays American antiques, and features a giant photomural at the entrance which further dramatizes the current harvest.

Restaurant: Summer Garden
Location: New York, New York
Designer: John Harding
Firm: Restaurant Associates Industries
Printer: DLG Business Group
Specifications:
Size: 12″ x 11″ cover

When the designer of this menu was traveling in California, he discovered the colorful antique fruit crate labels that were used by growers and shippers in the 1920s and 1930s. He purchased a large quantity of them, and later decided to use them for the covers of the Summer Garden menus. The outdoor restaurant, specializing in California cuisine, was a natural for these historic, eyecatching labels. Twelve different crate labels were mounted on cover stock with die-cut slots for changeable menu inserts. Summer Garden is part of the Restaurant Associates group.

5
Institutional and Travel Menus

An institutional restaurant is one that exists not for its own
sake, but as a dining facility for some other entity.
The institutions represented here include restaurants affiliated
with schools, hospitals, corporations, country clubs, race tracks
and sports facilities, as well as travel-related restaurants such
as those in airports and hotels.
While this covers a wide spectrum, all of these types of
restaurants are noteworthy for their unique styles.
Corporations, with their impressive images, the elegance of
country clubs, and rugged sports-related restaurants offer
some of the menus included here.

Menu

HORS D'OEUVRES

Country Ham & Blue Cheese Turnovers
Shrimp Spread
Country Pâté
Cheese Asparagus
Vegetable and Cheese Torte

ENTREES

Lamb Curry
*Spicy cubes of lamb mixed with onions,
mushrooms, peppers and raisins.*
Chicken Oriental
*A unique casserole of chicken, snow peas,
mushrooms, artichokes, water chestnuts,
onions . . . in a light cream sauce.*
Beef Bourguignon
*A hearty Provincial beef stew flavored with
mushrooms, onions, herbs and red wine.*
Parsley-Sesame Chicken
*A whole chicken breast coated with parsley and
sesame seeds, sautéed in lemon butter. Served
with a shallot sour cream sauce.*
Pasta Salads
*A variety of combinations using vegetables,
chicken and seafood. Changes daily.*
Chicken Salad
*Fresh herbs and homemade mayonnaise make
this one of the best.*

DESSERTS

Chocolate Velvet
Gâteau Nanni
Oatmeal Cake
Rum-Fudge Brownies
Carrot Cake
Chocolate Amaretto Truffles
Orange Ice

SOUPS & BREADS

Potato Mushroom Soup
Tomato Carrot Soup
French Bread
Whole Wheat Baguettes

CATERING

La Pêche offers a
complete catering ser-
vice to accommodate
any size party. In addi-
tion to catering, special
orders are available. We
are glad to satisfy any
gourmet request.

Fresh food is made
daily; call for daily
menus. Any item from
our previous menus is
also available.

SPECIALTIES

Béarnaise Sauce
Poppy Seed Dressing
Mayonnaise
Vinaigrette Salad Dressing, M.F.D.
Fudge Sauce

ENTERTAINING

La Pêche makes entertaining easy: stop by on your
way home from work for your last minute needs.
You can also stop by for a carry-out lunch or let us
drop it by. There is a delivery charge.

la pêche

La Pêche

Gourmet to Go
& Catering
1147 Bardstown Road
Louisville, Ky. 40204
(502) 451-0377

Hours:
Tuesday-Friday
10 until 6
Saturday
10 until 4

Available
daily for
January,
February
& March

Restaurant: La Pêche

Location: Louisville, Kentucky

Designer: Walter McCord

Firm: Walter McCord Graphic Design

Illustrator: Dover clip art illustration

Printer: Hamilton Printing

Specifications: Four Menus

Size: 11″ x 16½″ x 16½″ (3); 10″ x 15½″ (1)

Paper: Strathmore Artlaid, Americana, and Simpson Gainsborough

La Pêche began as a gourmet shop, but now has expanded into a sit-down cafe. La Pêche also functions as a catering service. The owner, Kathy Cary, studied cooking at Le Cordon Bleu in Paris, and her training is reflected in the exciting menu offerings.

The menu changes two to three times a year, and several thousand copies are printed each time. The large quantity reduces production costs considerably. Why such large quantities? Because the owner stongly believes in using the menu as a marketing tool. It is used as a mailing promotion to customers, left on the counter for take-outs, used as a poster, and put on bulletin boards. Old steel-engraved artwork and exciting silhouettes were obtained from Dover clip art.

La Pêche
Gourmet to Go
& Catering
1147 Bardstown Road
Louisville, Ky. 40204
(502) 451-0377

We offer a complete catering service to accommodate any size party. In addition to catering, special orders are available. We are glad to satisfy any gourmet request.

Fresh food is made daily; call for daily menus. Any item from our previous menus is also available.

We make entertaining easy: stop by on your way home from work for your last minute needs. You can also stop by for a carry-out lunch or let us drop it by. There is a delivery charge.

Available daily for August, September and October.

Hors d'oeuvres

Parmesan Cheese Puffs
Chicken Liver Paté
Spinach Herb Won Tons
Shrimp Spread

Entrées

Eggplant Parmesan
Sauteed eggplant layered with a thick tomato sauce and three kinds of cheese.

Chicken Tetrazzini
A fettucini and chicken casserole flavored with almonds and parmesan.

Rib-eye with Duxelles de Champignons
A rib-eye stuffed with mushrooms and shallots that have been simmered in wine. Topped with a mustard butter.

Mushroom and Chicken Crêpes
Stuffed and rolled crêpes topped with a cheddar sauce.

Pasta Salads
A variety of combinations using vegetables, chicken and seafood. Changes daily.

Chicken Salad
Fresh herbs and homemade mayonnaise make this one of the best.

*Veal Birds
(special order)
Veal scallops stuffed with prosciutto and cheese and served in a sour cream-mushroom sauce.

French Bread
Whole Wheat Baguettes

Desserts

Chocolate Velvet
Grapefruit Ice
Chocolate Chip Meringue Cookies
La Pêche Chocolate Brownies
Lemon-Apricot Squares
Ice Cream à la Pêche
Chocolate Mousse
Cheesecake
Carrot Cake

La Pêche Specialities

Bearnaise Sauce
Poppy Seed Dressing
Mayonnaise
Vinaigrette Salad Dressing

Restaurant: La Pêche
Location: Louisville, Kentucky
Designer: Walter McCord
Firm: Walter McCord Graphic Design
Illustrator: Dover clip art illustration
Printer: Hamilton Printing
Specifications: Four Menus
Size: 11″ x 16½″ x 16½″ (3);
10″ x 15½″ (1)
Paper: Strathmore Artlaid, Americana, and
Simpson Gainsborough

Restaurant: Rudi's Country Kitchen
Location: Big Indian, New York
Designer: Milton Glaser
Firm: Milton Glaser, Inc.
Illustrator: Milton Glaser
Printer: Metropolitan Printing
Specifications:
Size: 8″ x 12½″

Sophisticated interpretations of "health foods" are offered in a very attractive country setting at Rudi's Country Kitchen. Natural ingredients, many homegrown and freshly prepared, are the bases for most of the dishes. Clientele ranges from locals of the Woodstock region who appreciate wholesome foods interestingly prepared, to tourists driving through the Catskills region who are attracted by the restaurant's beautiful terrace and gardens. The menu is clearly organized, containing brief descriptions of significant ingredients or cooking techniques. Rudi was a spiritual teacher and it is his profile that is seen on the company trademark.

APPETIZERS

Lobster crepe with Mornay sauce	2.00
Clams casino	1.50
A fiesta of fresh seasonal fruits	.90
Fresh Louisiana shrimp cocktail	3.00
Fresh lump crabmeat cocktail	3.25
Escargot chablisienne	1.85
Iced fresh oysters on the half shell (in season)	2.00
Shrimp scampi	3.00
Mushrooms stuffed with crabmeat, Rive Gauche	2.00

THE LEFT BANK SAMPLER
Includes shrimp scampi, clams casino, and
stuffed mushrooms   3.50

SOUPS

from the tureen...steaming or iced

An excellent baked French onion soup, au gratin

Soup du jour

Jellied consomme madrilene

Chilled vichyssoise

CHAMPAGNES & SPARKLING WINES

Bin	½ Bottle	Bottle
CHAMPAGNE - Imported		
70 Dom Perignon		50.00
71 Taittinger Blanc De Blancs Brut		40.00
72 Bollinger Brut		22.00
73 Mumm's Cordon Rouge Brut		30.00
American		
74 Great Western Extra Dry Split 3.00	5.50	10.00
SPARKLING BURGUNDY - Imported		
75 Chauvenet Red Cap		16.00
American		
76 Great Western	5.50	10.00
		Split 3.00
OTHER SPARKLING WINES		
77 Asti Spumante		11.00
78 Royal Seal Cold Duck No. 1 N. Y. S.		6.00

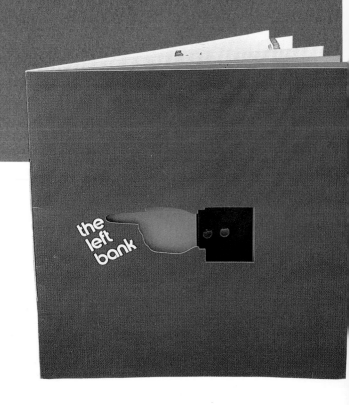

the left bank

Stuffed Lobster Tails
Filled with our savory lump crabmeat dressing,
and served with drawn butter **10.00**
We recommend our fine Pouilly Fuisse (Bin 47) or
Madrigal Moselle (Bin 55)

Broiled South African Lobster Tails
With fresh lemon wedge and drawn butter **10.00**
Delightful with Grand Cru Chablis (Bin 45) or B & G's
Puligny Montrachet (Bin 46)

King Crabmeat Casserole
Tender crabmeat, sauteed and served in its own
delightful butter sauce **6.95**
Delightful, too, with Madrigal Moselle (Bin 55), or
Paul Masson's Chablis (Bin 50)

Baked Deviled Crabs
Delicate crabmeat, blended with herbs and
spices, baked and served with
mustard sauce **6.50**
Enjoy this with Pouilly Fuisse (Bin 47) or
B & G Prince D'Argent (Bin 48)

Left Bank Stuffed Shrimp
Filled with savory lump crabmeat
dressing, and baked to a
golden brown **8.50**
We recommend a fine imported
Bordeaux (Bin 40, 41 or 42)

Baked Crabmeat Imperial
Fresh lump crabmeat in a delicious sauce,
baked a-bubbling, and served with fresh
lemon wedges **6.75**
We recommend our Graacher Himmelrich Moselle
(Bin 54)...or perhaps a little Blue Nun? (Bin 53)

Restaurant: The Left Bank
Location: Wilkes Barre, Pennsylvania
Designer: Lew Lehrman
Firm: Design Unlimited/Culinary Concepts
Printer: East Coast Lithographers
Die-cuts: Freedman Cutouts
Specifications: Dinner Menu with Wine List
Size: 11" x 11"

"Something different" was requested for the design of this menu for a Treadways Inn restaurant. The result, printed on duplex paper, shows an imaginative use of die-cuts to build upon one another. Old steel engravings were used as decorative motifs throughout. By displaying wine suggestions at the end of each entree listing, this fine dining menu helps the customers order wisely by educating them as to which wines blend the best with which foods. Consequently, this well-planned menu sells more wine, while maximizing the patron's dining pleasure.

Restaurant: The Hemisphere Club
Location: New York, New York
Designer: Time, Inc., in-house staff
Produced by: Restaurant Associates Industries
Printer: Tribune Lithographers
Specifications:
Size: 7" x 5¾"

This menu was designed for the private lunch club at Time, Inc., in the tower suite of the Time-Life building, which is used exclusively for corporate entertainment. A hand-lettered logo on rich colored stock elegantly enhances the strong corporate image.

Restaurant: Racquets Restaurant and Bar
Location: Forest Hills, New York
Designer: Restaurant Associates Industries in-house staff
Printer: DLG Business Group
Specifications:
Size: 7" x 1¾"

Racquets, a 170-seat, three-tier restaurant overlooking the grandstand court of Forest Hills Stadium in Flushing Meadows, features a variety of quality ethnic foods. Classically elegant, with crossed tennis racquets and ball for the logo, entry selections are headed with tennis-related terms. Racquets is part of the Restaurant Associates group.

RACQUETS
Restaurant & Bar
1982

WARM UP VOLLEY
Shrimp Cocktail	6.75
Roulade of Striped Bass with Morels	4.50
Cranshaw Melon	3.95
Chilled Tomato Orange Bisque	3.95

'THE OPEN' PANTRY
Seafood Salad (Scallops, Shrimp, Lobster Chunks, King Crab Meat)	15.50
Smoked Scotch Salmon, Pumpernickel, Cucumber Salad	13.50
Breast of Chicken Salad Louis with Pineapple Sticks	11.95
Chilled Tortellini Salad Primavera	11.95
Baseline Chef Salad (Mixed Greens, Ham, Turkey, Salami, Swiss Cheese, Mushrooms)	11.50

ADVANTAGE GRILL
New York Cut Sirloin Steak, Maitre D'Hotel Butter	18.95
Broiled Double Lamb Chops, Watercress	17.50
Center Cut Swordfish Steak, Anchovy Butter	17.50
Prime Rib of Beef Au Jus	17.95
Seafood Lasagne	16.25

SPECIALS
Chef's Special (Changes Daily)	15.95
Catch of the Day (Daily Fresh Fish, Baked or Poached)	15.95

All items above served with Roast Potatoes and Fresh Vegetable of the Day

MATCH POINT
Fresh Fruit Salad	2.95
Tartufo	2.95
Vanilla Ice Cream, Raspberry Sauce	3.25
Cheese Cake	3.25
Chocolate Mousse Cake	3.25
Fresh Strawberries in Cream	3.95
Coffee	.85

DINNER

RESTAURANT ASSOCIATES INDUSTRIES, INC.

Restaurant: Trumpet's
Location: New York, New York
Designer: Frank Burstin
Firm: Concord Press, Inc.
Printer: Concord Press, Inc.
Specifications: Dinner Menu and Supper Card
Size: 12″ x 16½″ flat card;
9½″ x 15″ dinner menu
Paper: Strathmore Grandee

Trumpet's clientele consists mainly of corporate business accounts attracted to its midtown location in the Grand Hyatt Hotel near Grand Central Station.

A slight departure from the classic fine dining menu, Trumpet's still retains an elegant contemporary look. The logo is die-cut and gold foil-stamped. There are separate menus for dinner, supper, and dessert. The menus are mounted on heavy boards for extra thickness. Trumpet's dessert menu is featured in the Specialty chapter.

Restaurant: Marriott Host
Location: Large airport lounges across the U.S.
Designer: Larry McAdams
Firm: Larry McAdams Design, Inc.
Illustrator: Bob Krogle
Specifications: Airport Lounge Drink Menu
Size: 6″ x 10″
Paper: Hopper Chambray

This slick "Just Plane Fun" menu is distributed in the lounges of some of the larger airports. Die-cut windows open to display drinks held by a stewardess inside. The menu may be adapted to accommodate different printed inserts offering drink selections.

Restaurant: Charlie's
Location: Atlantic City, New Jersey
Designer: Lee Blumberg
Firm: L.J. Blumberg Company, Inc.
Specifications:
Size: 9″ x 12″

Located in the Golden Nugget Hotel Casino, Charlie's features an elegant burgundy velvet menu cover with a handsome steel-engraved logo; the restaurant's European-style interior also contains touches of burgundy velvet. The menu, offering impressive cuts of dry aged prime beef and fine seafood, is notably well organized and easy to read. The interior pages of the menu are gold foil-stamped with a design.

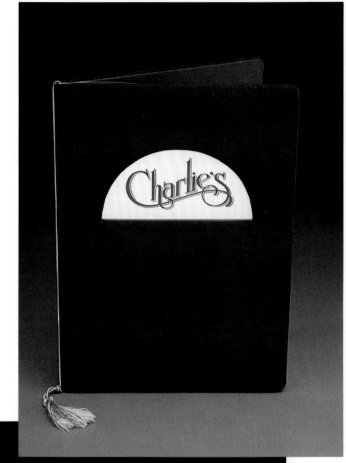

Congratulations!

Restaurant: St. Luke's Hospital
Location: Boise, Idaho
Designer: Dennis Chase
Illustrator: Dennis Chase
Printer: Joslyn Morris, Inc.
Specifications: Celebration Menu
Size: 4½″ x 11½″
Paper: Linen stock

This "celebration" menu is presented in the maternity ward to new mothers. The menu contains a loose insert personalized with the handwritten names of the mother and newborn child. It is printed with blue and gold metallic ink on a linen stock.

Restaurant: Pan American Airways
Location: In-Flight Food Service
Designer: Ivan Chermayeff
Firm: Chermayeff & Geismar Associates
Illustrator: Ivan Chermayeff
Specifications:
Size: Drink Menu (blue) 5½″ x 9¼″
Food Menu (white) 8½″ x 14″

Pan Am's menus for passengers in flight sets up an evocative dining experience, while stimulating expected experiences of foreign places. Airline passengers always seeking to pass the time, have time to read, and this menu is meant to be studied slowly and contemplated. The calligraphy evokes an interesting blend of international cities. The artist has left little space between the names of the cities, and they all seem to blend together into one integrated design. The loose flourishes of the letters create a feeling of movement. The French menus supply short English translations where necessary.

Restaurant: Victoria's
Location: Atlantic City, New Jersey
Designer: Lee Blumberg
Firm: L.J. Blumberg Co. Inc
Specifications:
Size: 9″ x 12″

Victoria's, which specializes in continental cuisine, is one of the restaurants at the Golden Nugget Hotel Casino, and is known as the finest hotel dining facility in the area. The menu is in keeping with the Victorian style and ambiance of the dining room. The cloth brocade cover compliments the dining room's decor, which is primarily in shades of green.

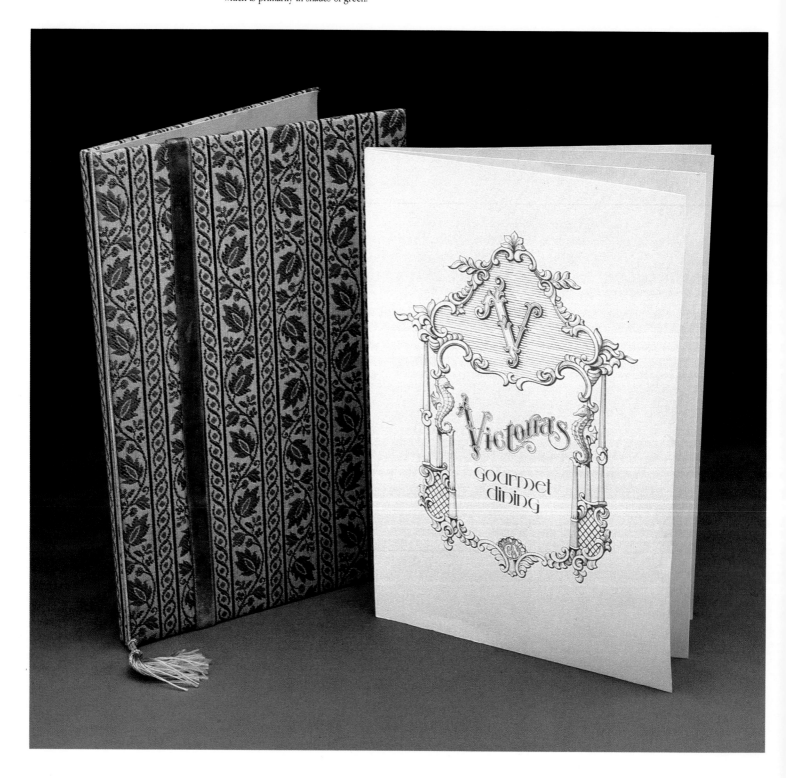

Restaurant: Point O' Woods
Location: Benton Harbor, Michigan
Designer: Lew Lehrman
Firm: Design Unlimited/Culinary Concepts
Illustrator: Robin Smith
Printer: East Coast Lithographers
Specifications:
Size: 10" x 7"
Paper: Hammermill Cover

This menu for the dining room of a country club depicts a golf course scene on the front cover along with the distinctive Point O' Woods logo. The wine list is included with the food menu, and other illustrated scenes of the country club appear inside.

6

Specialty Menus

Desserts and beverages are not the only items that can merit
a specialty menu all their own. Among the menus collected
for this book were examples designed for burgers, appetizers,
hors d'ouevres, soup, and separate drink lists for coffees, soft
drinks, wine, and alcohol.

Desserts and beverages can provide a considerable profit for
the restaurant, due to the large percentage of mark-up. For
example, a wedge of cake may sell for $3.50. Ten of these
wedges could be cut from the same cake, yielding $35, which
may represent a 300% profit. What about a soft drink that
costs the restaurant approximately 25¢ per glass to make and
sells for $1.50? Or mixed alcoholic beverages? These are
high profit items as they take very little preparation time and
can be served quickly. Giving these items their own menu
space sells more of them by sheer emphasis.

Restaurant: Port of Italy
Location: Temple Hills, Maryland
Designer: Lew Lehrman
Firm: Design Unlimited/Culinary Concepts
Illustrator: Design Unlimited/Culinary Concepts
Printer: Artisan Printers
Die-Cutter: Freedman Cut-outs
Specifications: Dessert and Beverage Menu
Size: Stands 6″ high
Paper: Simpson Sundance Felt Cover 80#

Port of Italy has modeled their three-dimensional, die-cut tabletop menu after the old-fashioned Italian dessert cart that stands in the dining room. The traditional red, white, and green colors add Italian flavor. The reverse side of this menu lists coffees and liqueurs. The restaurant's main menu is featured in the chapter on Ethnic Dining.

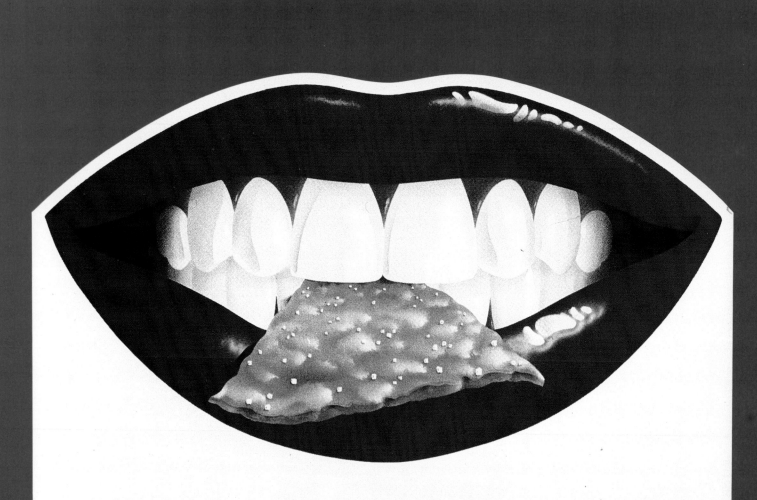

EL TORITO®
Cantina Appetizers

Restaurant: El Torito

Location: Nationwide chain headquartered in Irvine, California

Designer: Larry McAdams

Firm: Larry McAdams Design, Inc.

Illustrator: Larry McAdams

Specifications: Appetizer menu

Size: 6″ x 6½″

Paper: Kromecoat

A sensual mouth nibbling a nacho tortilla chip appears on the front and back covers of the mini appetizer menu, which features four selections.

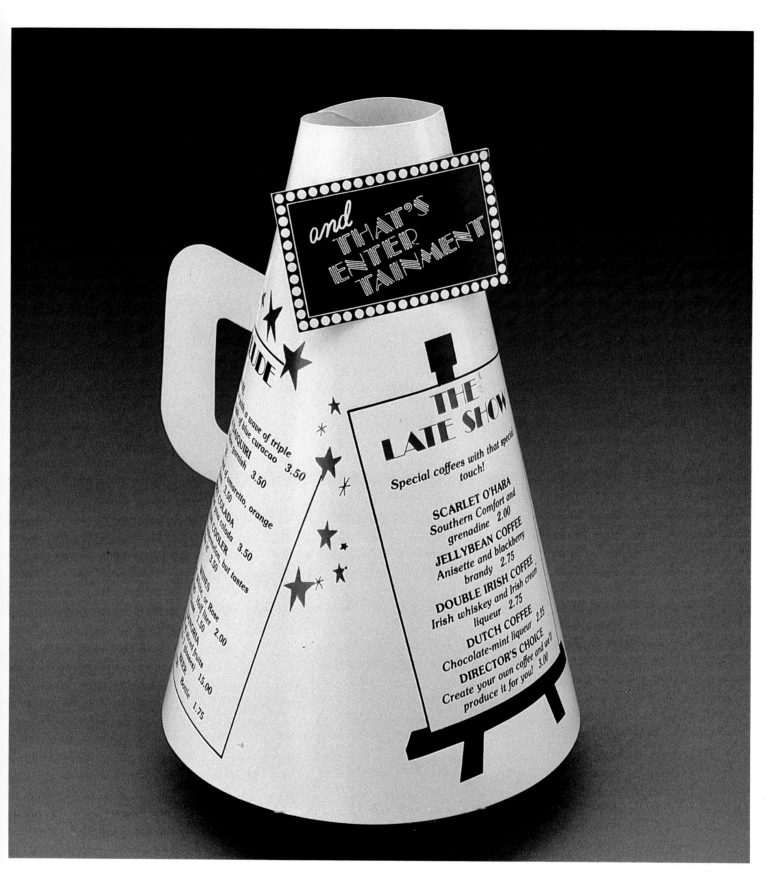

Restaurant: And That's Entertainment

Location: Montgomery, Alabama

Designer: Lew Lehrman

Firm: Design Unlimited/Culinary Concepts

Printer: East Coast Lithographers

Specifications: Beverage List

Size: stands 7¼″

This three-dimensional, die-cut megaphone ties in with the restaurant's theatrical theme. The menu features alcoholic shakes, special coffees, and other assorted beverages. The megaphone is an entertaining conversation piece—but watch out, it really works! The main menu for this restaurant is featured in the Theme chapter.

Restaurant: Sundae's
Location: Atlantic City, New Jersey
Designer: Lew Lehrman
Firm: Design Unlimited/Culinary Concepts
Photographer: Jay Brenner Studios
Printer: Sterling Roman Press
Die Cutter: Freedman Cutouts
Specifications: Ice Cream Menu
Size: 9½" x 9½"
Paper: Kromecoat

As with most casino/hotel assignments, the cost of producing a menu was no object, thus enabling the designer to do precisely what was needed to satisfy the client, Bally's Park Place Casino and Hotel. This flamboyant "Busby Berkley-type" production recreates with maximum impact an ice cream eating experience. The full-color cover displays clean, appetizing shots of ice cream confections. The menu opens to a realistic, life-sized pop-up of mouthwatering sundaes.

Restaurant: Bennigan's Tavern
Location: Nationwide chain
Designer: Rex Peteet
Firm: Dennard Creative
Creative Director: Bob Dennard
Illustrator: Rex Peteet
Copywriters: Bob Dennard and Glyn Powell
Printer: Jarvis Press
Specifications: Hamburger Menu
Size: 6" x 11¾"
Paper: Kromecoat

The designer and copywriter for Bennigan's burger menu obviously had fun with this one. Bennigan's claims, on the front of their menu, that this burger will change your life. People become better citizens, better dressers, even better lovers! They say they've sold over a zillion trillion hamburgers (and that's more than you know who).The ingenious pull-out on the top of the pickle opens to reveal a special choice of toppings, each illustrated and described.

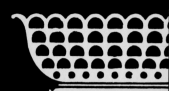

A BURGER YOU CAN BELIEVE IN

They said it couldn't be done. A burger so juicy, so scrumptious, so incredibly delicious that it could earn the Bennigan's name. Introducing the Bennigan's Burger. A burger you can believe in. So tantalizingly tasty it changes peoples lives. Makes them better citizens. Better lovers. Better dressers. It's the burger you thought they gave up trying to make years ago. Well think again, bubba. It's here. And it's incredible. We've already sold a couple of trillion, maybe a zillion trillion. You believe that?

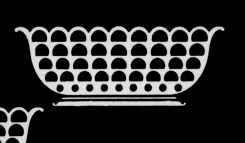

The Bennigan's Burger comes with lettuce, tomato, onion and pickle spear. You can choose from seven incredibly delicious toppings. Each only $3.95. And that you can believe.

WITH AMERICAN CHEESE. So absolutely incredible you'll want to stand up and salute. Maybe even join the Army.

WITH SAUTEED ONIONS. So wonderful it will bring tears to your eyes.

WITH SWISS CHEESE AND BACON. So delectable you'll probably yodel or oink! Maybe both. Yodelaaaaeeeeoink!

WITH SWISS CHEESE AND CANADIAN BACON. So scrumptious it can move Mounties. Even a battalion of them.

WITH SWISS CHEESE AND GUACAMOLE. (California style.) So mucho delicioso it'll have you speaking Spanish backwards. Elomacaug!

WITH CHILI. Ay ya ya! So bueno you'll think you're in Chihauhua. Would you believe Terlingua, Texas?

WITH SAUTEED MUSHROOMS. Ooh la la! So deliciously French, you'll want to join the Foreign Legion.

Or for a little extra you can have your choice of french fries, fresh fruit or a cup of soup of the day with your Bennigan's Burger. Only $4.45. Unbelievable.

Restaurant: Gadgets
Location: East Rutherford, New Jersey
Designer: Lew Lehrman
Firm: Design Unlimited/Culinary Concepts
Illustrator: Bill Kresse
Printer: East Coast Lithographers
Die-cutter: Freedman Cutouts
Specifications: Drink List
Size: 3½" x 9¼"

This die-cut, three dimensional, stand-up menu is hilariously silly—as is the general Looney Tunes™ theme of the restaurant. Drinks, ostensibly prepared by a crew of mad scientists, are served in pyrex laboratory beakers, with laboratory straws. With entries referred to as "elixirs," "concoctions," and "potions," this menu will entertain patrons as they make their drink selections. Gadget's children's menu is featured in the Children's chapter.

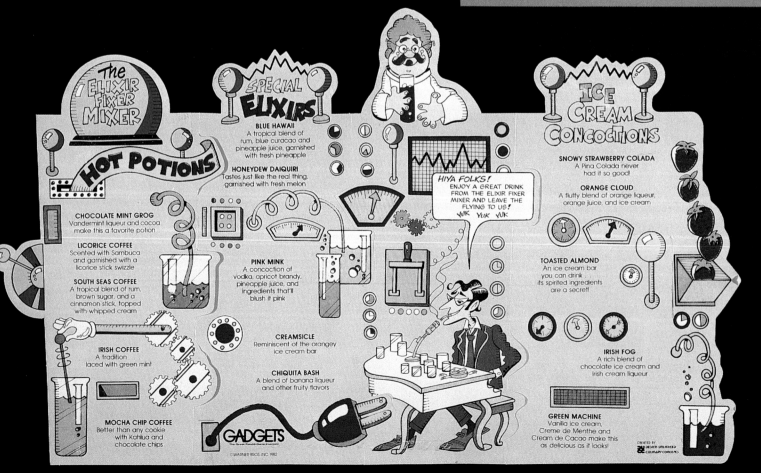

Restaurant: Bennigan's Tavern

Location: Nationwide chain headquartered in Dallas, Texas

Designer: Glyn Powell

Firm: Dennard Creative

Creative Director: Bob Dennard

Calligrapher: Glyn Powell

Printer: Yaquinto Printing

Specifications: Toast Beverage Menu

Size: 5″ x 8¼″

Paper: Speckletone

This eating establishment caters largely to young people. Bennigan's menu was created to help promote their hot winter drinks. Along with interesting drink entries, the menu contains a humorous list of suggested toasts as good conversation starters. The toasts were taken from the book *Toasts* by Paul Dickson

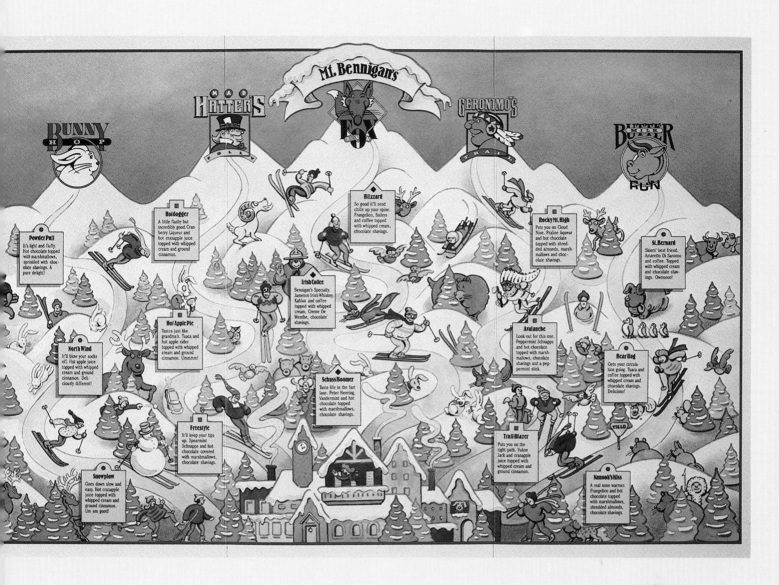

Restaurant:	Bennigan's Tavern
Location:	Nationwide chain headquartered in Dallas, Texas
Designer:	Don Sibley
Firm:	Dennard Creative
Illustrator:	Jerry Jeanmard
Printer:	Williamson Printing
Specifications:	Winter Drink Menu
Size:	6¾″ x 12¾″
Paper:	Lustro Offset Enamel Dull White

Bennigan's winter drink menu is sure to warm any cold day. This brilliantly colored menu opens to a hilarious animated scene on the ski slopes. The drink entries are written on the mountains, in ski-slope lingo. The potency of the drinks are rated easiest, more difficult, and most difficult.

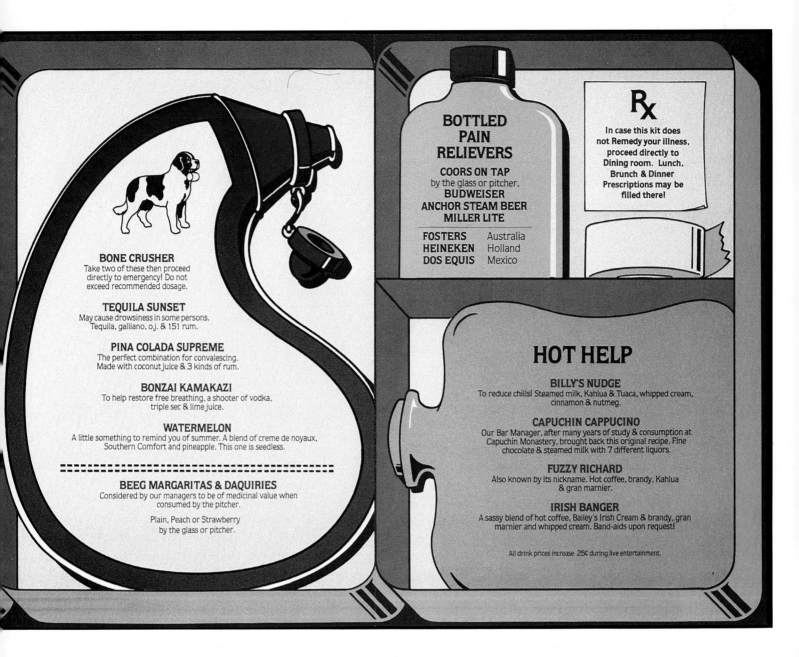

BONE CRUSHER
Take two of these then proceed
directly to emergency! Do not
exceed recommended dosage.

TEQUILA SUNSET
May cause drowsiness in some persons.
Tequila, galliano, o.j. & 151 rum.

PINA COLADA SUPREME
The perfect combination for convalescing.
Made with coconut juice & 3 kinds of rum.

BONZAI KAMAKAZI
To help restore free breathing, a shooter of vodka,
triple sec & lime juice.

WATERMELON
A little something to remind you of summer. A blend of creme de noyaux,
Southern Comfort and pineapple. This one is seedless.

BEEG MARGARITAS & DAQUIRIES
Considered by our managers to be of medicinal value when
consumed by the pitcher.

Plain, Peach or Strawberry
by the glass or pitcher.

**BOTTLED
PAIN
RELIEVERS**

COORS ON TAP
by the glass or pitcher.
**BUDWEISER
ANCHOR STEAM BEER
MILLER LITE**

FOSTERS	Australia
HEINEKEN	Holland
DOS EQUIS	Mexico

Rx
In case this kit does
not Remedy your illness,
proceed directly to
Dining room. Lunch,
Brunch & Dinner
Prescriptions may be
filled there!

HOT HELP

BILLY'S NUDGE
To reduce chills! Steamed milk, Kahlua & Tuaca, whipped cream,
cinnamon & nutmeg.

CAPUCHIN CAPPUCINO
Our Bar Manager, after many years of study & consumption at
Capuchin Monastery, brought back this original recipe. Fine
chocolate & steamed milk with 7 different liquors.

FUZZY RICHARD
Also known by its nickname. Hot coffee, brandy, Kahlua
& gran marnier.

IRISH BANGER
A sassy blend of hot coffee, Bailey's Irish Cream & brandy, gran
marnier and whipped cream. Band-aids upon request!

All drink prices increase .25¢ during live entertainment.

Restaurant:	J.P. Mac's
Location:	Huntington Beach, California
Designers:	Dave Tanimoto and Larry McAdams
Firm:	Larry McAdams Design, Inc.
Printer:	Precision Offset
Specifications:	Drink List
Size:	7″ x 10″

The West Coast restaurant serves California-style cuisine and features live country-western music. The crowd, generally young and casual, wanted a menu that was fun and clever. The result was this "Thirst Aid Kit" containing remedies in the form of "Bottled Pain Relievers," "Hot-Help," and other bar room pharmaceutical concoctions.

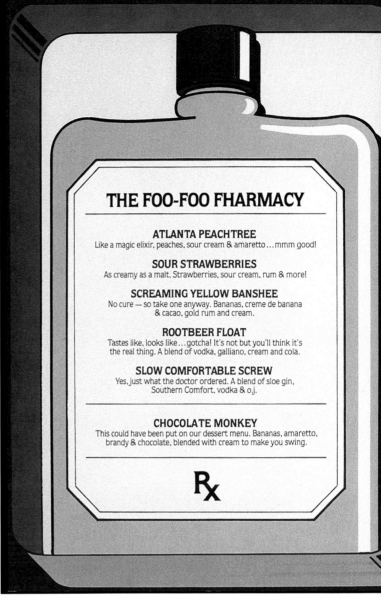

THE FOO-FOO FHARMACY

ATLANTA PEACHTREE
Like a magic elixir, peaches, sour cream & amaretto...mmm good!

SOUR STRAWBERRIES
As creamy as a malt. Strawberries, sour cream, rum & more!

SCREAMING YELLOW BANSHEE
No cure — so take one anyway. Bananas, creme de banana
& cacao, gold rum and cream.

ROOTBEER FLOAT
Tastes like, looks like...gotcha! It's not but you'll think it's
the real thing. A blend of vodka, galliano, cream and cola.

SLOW COMFORTABLE SCREW
Yes, just what the doctor ordered. A blend of sloe gin,
Southern Comfort, vodka & o.j.

CHOCOLATE MONKEY
This could have been put on our dessert menu. Bananas, amaretto,
brandy & chocolate, blended with cream to make you swing.

℞

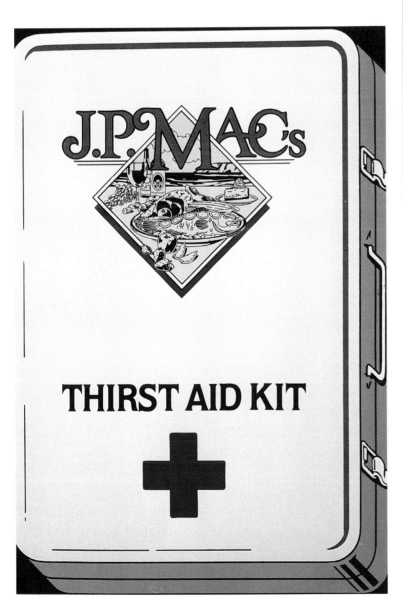

J.P.MAC's

THIRST AID KIT

Restaurant: T.G.I. Friday's
Location: Nationwide chain headquartered in Dallas, Texas
Designer: Woody Pirtle
Illustrators: Woody Pirtle and Don Grimes
Printer: Allcraft Printing
Specifications: T.G.I. Friday's Drink and Snack Bottle Menu
Size: 5¾" x 10¾"

A new twist on the liquor menu, T.G.I. Friday's has created its own die-cut liqueur bottle which opens to an array of tempting choices. The rich, shiny chocolate brown of the bottle is tastefully seductive.

STRAWBERRY & CHOCOLATE

STRAWBERRY DAIQUIRI
Made with Crushed Strawberries. Deep Red and Flavorful. (Also Peach and Banana)

STRAWBERRY PIÑA COLADA
Pineapple and Coconut Enhanced with the Real Berry.

STRAWBERRY MARGARITA
Strawberries Added to Tequila, Triple Sec and Lime For a Fruitier Flavor.

STRAWBERRY SHORTCAKE
A Creamy Mixture that Tastes Just Like a Strawberry Shortcake. Topped with Whipped Cream.

CHOCOLATE MONKEY
Like the Chocolate Covered Banana Sold at State Fairs.

GRASSHOPPER
Green Mint, White Creme de Cacao and Ice Cream.

ICE CREAM SANDWICH
Made with Chocolate Cream Cookies To Taste Like Its Name.

CHOCOLATE MINT
Very Chocolaty, Like a Cool, After-Dinner Mint.

ALL TIME FAVORITES

SNOW BEAR
Amaretto and Ice Cream Give This The Flavor of Old-Fashioned Vanilla.

PIÑA COLADA
Light Rum and Our Mix of Papaya, Fresh Orange Juice, Pineapple and Coconut.

PEACHES AND CREAM
Real Peaches, Ice Cream and Vodka. Thick and Creamy.

COCABANANA
An Ice Cream Drink with the Tropical Flavors of Banana and Coconut.

PEACH ALMOND SHAKE
Amaretto, Ice Cream and Real Peaches.

BANANA SPLIT
The Soda Fountain Favorite. Real Fruit and Ice Cream Blended with two Liqueurs and Creme de Cacao.

VELVET HAMMER
The Classic Combination of White Creme de Cacao, Triple Sec and Grenadine, Blended with Ice Cream.

FRIDAY'S MARTINI
Very Dry, Portioned Friday's Way. Also Manhattan, Old-Fashioned and the Gimlet Deluxe.

Restaurant: Sands Hotel Casino
Location: Atlantic City, New Jersey
Designer: Lew Lehrman
Firm: Design Unlimited/Culinary Concepts
Photographer: EPD Color Labs
Printer: Sterling Roman Press
Die-Cutter: Freedman Cutouts
Specifications: Dessert Menu
Size: stands 7¼″
Paper: 12 pt. Kromecoat, two sides

The Sands Hotel Casino used an actual photograph of a cake and ice cream for its three-dimensional tabletop menu. Dessert entries are printed directly on the photo. The photograph is so highly detailed that if you look closely, you can actually see the layers of the cake. The Sands caters to gamblers and fun-seekers who have high expectations in terms of service, amenities, and "glitz."

Restaurant: Gordon
Location: Chicago, Illinois
Designer: David Bartels
Firm: Bartels & Company
Illustrator: Gregg McNair
Printer: Art Craft Lithographers
Specifications: Wine List
Size: 6½" x 11"
Paper: Kromecoat

In this witty, award-winning menu for Gordon, a Greek column holding a feather and a wineglass that's about to tip over give clients plenty to wonder about. The pink logo was hand lettered by the designer. The restaurant serves continental cuisine to a predominantly business clientele.

Restaurant: The Great House
Location: Miami, Florida
Designer: Milton Glaser
Firm: Milton Glaser, Inc.
Illustrator: Milton Glaser
Printer: Metropolitan Printing
Specifications: Wine List
Size: 6″ x 14″
Paper: 80# Ivory Strathmore Pastelle Cover

This restaurant was conceptualized by Joseph Baum, designed by Phil George, and contains decorative elements and graphics by Milton Glaser, Inc. The Great House was originally conceived as the focal point of a new super-luxury condominium development. It was to have been a world-class restaurant in terms of quality of food, sumptuousness of interior, and scale of prices, and intended to serve only the residents of the condominium and their guests. As it turned out, most of the clientele preferrred a different sort of culinary experience and many changes were made to accommodate the demand for less formal cuisine. Menu graphics picked up on some of the decorative elements of the restaurant's etched-glass panels.

Restaurant: Sinclair's
Location: Lake Forest, Illinois
Designer: David Bartels
Firm: Bartels & Co.
Illustrator: Gregg McNair
Printer: Art Craft Lithographers
Specifications: Wine List
Size: 6½″ x 11″
Paper: Kromecoat

This menu design has won numerous national and international awards. The restaurant's patrons will get their money's worth with the humorous illustration of the tiny man running with a slightly oversize cork screw. Sinclair's specializes in American cooking and serves an upscale suburban clientele. Their main menu is featured in the Fine Dining section of this book.

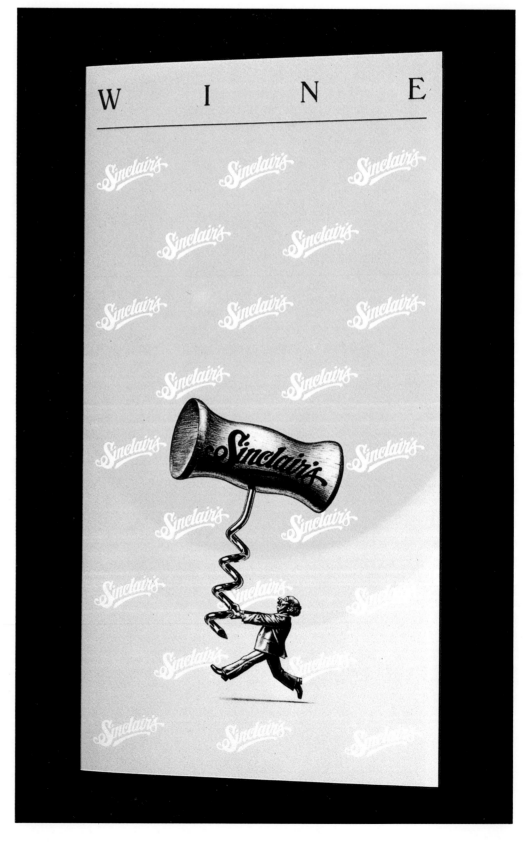

Restaurant: Dalts
Location: Nationwide chain owned by
T.G.I. Friday's, Inc., headquartered
in Dallas, Texas
Designer: Woody Pirtle
Firm: Pirtle Design
Illustrators: Woody Pirtle and Mike Schroeder
Printer: Allcraft Printing
Specifications: Dalts Drink Menu
Size: 4⅜″ x 9¾″

The restaurant's logo appears on a coaster actually
applied to the front cover. Ice cream drinks and
coffees are listed inside.

Restaurant: Radisson Corporation
Location: Minneapolis, Minnesota
Designer: Jac Coverdale
Firm: Clarity Coverdale Advertising
Photographer: Kent Severson
Printer: Associated Lithographers
Specifications: Drink List
Size: 9″ x 7″
Paper: 60# White Lustro Cover

This menu was designed for Radisson's upscale hotel restaurant clientele. Specifically intended as a "suggestive sell" drink menu for cocktail lounges to promote specialty drinks, close-up photography across spreads was used to help produce a visually satisfying drinking experience. You can almost feel the cold drink splashing into the glass, smell the luscious tropical fruits, and taste the tart Alamo. The Alamo glass is advertised on the menu as a retail item.

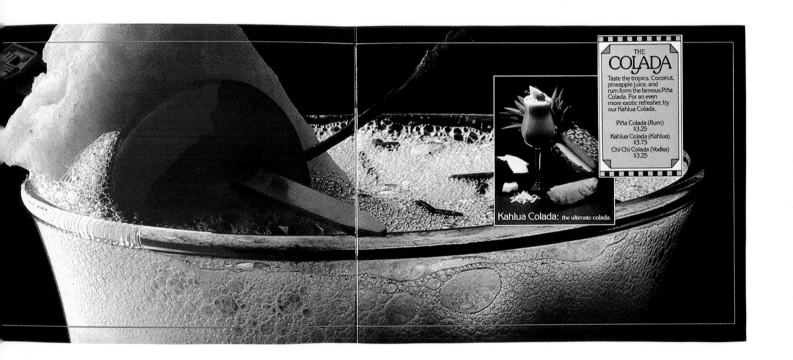

Restaurant: All Seasons
Location: Atlanta, Georgia
Designer: Robin Smith
Firm: Design Unlimited/Culinary Concepts
Illustrator: Robin Smith
Printer: Artisan Printers
Die-Cutter: Freedman Cutouts
Specifications: Dessert and Drink Menu
Size: 7¼″ x 9¾″
Paper: Beckett Cover, double thick

All Seasons' three-dimensional die-cut tabletop menu is a flower pot filled with flowers. Any way the menu turns, the restaurant's name is clearly visible. Each flower contains a beverage or dessert entry along with the price. All Seasons is located in a Howard Johnson's motel.

Restaurant: Bennigan's Tavern
Location: Nationwide chain headquartered in Dallas, Texas
Designer: Don Sibley
Firm: Dennard Creative
Creative Director: Bob Dennard
Illustrators: Don Sibley and Rex Peteet
Printer: Riverside Press
Specifications: Passport Menu
Size: 5½″ x 8½″
Paper: Mixed stock

Summer is the time to take vacations and travel, and this summertime drink menu is the "passport to paradise." Each page features drinks from the country whose visa is stamped on the top of that page.

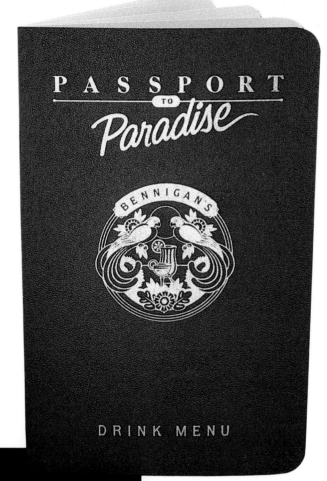

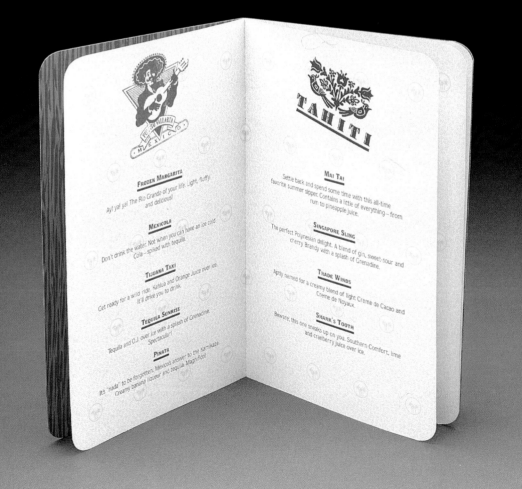

Make It S

T *he enticing rainbow of*
chocolate desserts enjoye
the Aztecs and Mayans
served at Montezuma's court, ha
vividly recorded by Friar Bernadir
Sahagun.

In fact, these male domin
societies considered their delect
desserts "too good" for women, and only men were
allowed to eat chocolate and many other sweets. I
Eighteenth Century, Spanish nuns introduced ev
more variety to Mexico's wealth of desserts and at
women too, began enjoying them.

At Plata Grande, all desserts, save ice cre
are home made and each is highly recommended
ladies and gentlemen alike.

Restaurant: Plata Grande Restaurant
Location: Beltsville, Maryland
Designers: Kathleen Wilmes Herring
and Michael David Brown
Firm: MDB Communications, Inc.
Printer: Peake Printers, Inc.
Specifications: Dessert Menu
Size: 10" x 13"
Paper: Strathmore Grandee, Pyrenees White,
80# Cover

Plata Grande's dessert menu offers a wide variety of unusual Mexican specialty desserts, including fried ice cream and sautéed plantains. Detailed descriptions of desserts are included. The menu contains some good silly humor, as well as Dayglo-colored ice cream, lots of guns and bullets, and a bandito, about to be executed, with green ice cream on his tongue. This menu is considered to be directly responsible for an increase in dessert sales. The restaurant's main menu is featured in the Ethnic Dining chapter.

Por Favor

el De Queso Y Lima ▪▶ Home made, cheesecake the way only our home can ..e it—with cream cheese, brandy, and a ..shing taste of lime. $1.65

a Zanahoria ▪▶ A three-layer tropical ..t cake mountain, molded with nuts, ..s, dates, cream cheese, coconut and ..nds. And the vanilla mocha butter ..n icing? A true mountaintop experience! ..5

▪▶ This is the traditional version of ..er popular carmel sauced egg custard. ..e made of course. $1.25

..alla ▪▶ Egg custard garnished with ..ge slices, strawberries, and syrup. (Made ..haring) $2.95

..Hojas ▪▶ A "thousand leaves" of ..d puff pastry filled with vanilla cream, ..guaranteed to melt in your mouth. ..0

..e Granita ▪▶ A very light secret icy ..rt (all we'll mention is the coffee and ..), topped with whipped cream. Mysteri- ..nd magnifica! $1.40

..illitas Carlotta ▪▶ Vanilla ice cream ..ed with sugar-sprinkled fried flour ..lla strips, and topped with strawberries ..whipped cream. You'll think you're ..ming. $2.50

Chocolate Con Ceresas ▪▶ A four-layer chocolate cake masterpiece, sprinkled with cherry heering and liberally covered with chocolate butter cream. $1.85

Fried Ice Cream ▪▶ First we wrap ice cream in a fine leafy pastry dough. Roll it lightly in cinnamon, and then we fry it. A dab of honey and a dollop of whipped cream and then we dash it out to you. $1.95

Sopapillas ▪▶ Fried and puffy heavenly home made buttermilk pastry dough. Served with whipped honey and cinnamon butter. $1.45

Platanos Tropical ▪▶ Fresh sliced bananas sauteed in sugar, butter, and guava jelly. Served flambe, over vanilla ice cream. An absolute vision! (Made for Sharing) $3.95

Ice Cream ▪▶ One perfect bowl, brim- ming with creamy Vanilla or selected special flavors. $1.25

Mexican Mud Pie ▪▶ Three kinds of ice cream, layers of fudge and carmel—are the basic ingredients that are combined to build a chocolate cookie crusted frozen pie. This is an unbelievable treat. One look will convince you that you can not eat the whole piece. One Taste and You Will! $2.25

Potable Postre

Mexican Coffee
Piping hot coffee enlivened with three smooth spirits. One is Creme de Noyaux, and the other two? Use your imagination! Topped with whipped cream, and a minia- ture Mexican flag. After all, the taste is a national celebration. $1.95

Cafe Villa
A glowing cupful of cocoa, Amaretto, and steaming coffee topped with whipped cream. $2.10

Cappuccino
A scintillating blend of cocoa, brandy and steaming coffee, crowned with whipped cream. $2.10

Crema Del Los Mayas
Cool off and mellow out with a tantalizing blend of Kahlua, Triple Sec, and cream on the rocks. $2.20

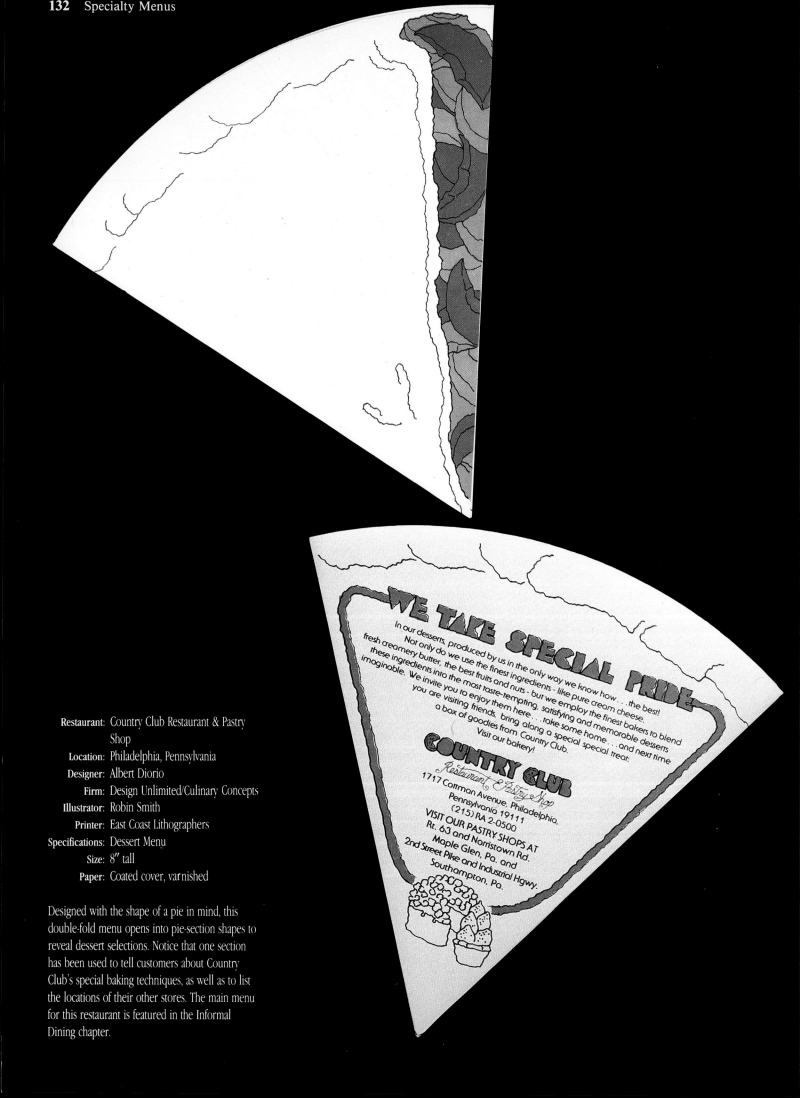

WE TAKE SPECIAL PRIDE

In our desserts, produced by us in the only way we know how...the best!
Not only do we use the finest ingredients - like pure cream cheese,
fresh creamery butter, the best fruits and nuts - but we employ the finest bakers to blend
these ingredients into the most taste-tempting, satisfying and memorable desserts
imaginable. We invite you to enjoy them here...take some home...and next time
you are visiting friends, bring along a special special treat:
a box of goodies from Country Club.
Visit our bakery!

COUNTRY CLUB
Restaurant & Pastry Shop
1717 Cottman Avenue, Philadelphia,
Pennsylvania 19111
(215) RA 2-0500
VISIT OUR PASTRY SHOPS AT
Rt. 63 and Norristown Rd.
Maple Glen, Pa. and
2nd Street Pike and Industrial Hgwy.
Southampton, Pa.

Restaurant: Country Club Restaurant & Pastry
Shop
Location: Philadelphia, Pennsylvania
Designer: Albert Diorio
Firm: Design Unlimited/Culinary Concepts
Illustrator: Robin Smith
Printer: East Coast Lithographers
Specifications: Dessert Menu
Size: 8″ tall
Paper: Coated cover, varnished

Designed with the shape of a pie in mind, this
double-fold menu opens into pie-section shapes to
reveal dessert selections. Notice that one section
has been used to tell customers about Country
Club's special baking techniques, as well as to list
the locations of their other stores. The main menu
for this restaurant is featured in the Informal
Dining chapter.

Restaurant: Trumpet's
Location: New York, New York
Designer: Frank Burstin
Firm: Concord Press, Inc.
Printer: Concord Press
Specifications: Dessert Menu
Size: 9″ x 12″
Paper: Strathmore

Trumpet's dessert menu has an elegant contemporary look. The logo is die-cut and gold foil-stamped. There is a separate dinner menu which is featured in the Institutional Dining chapter.

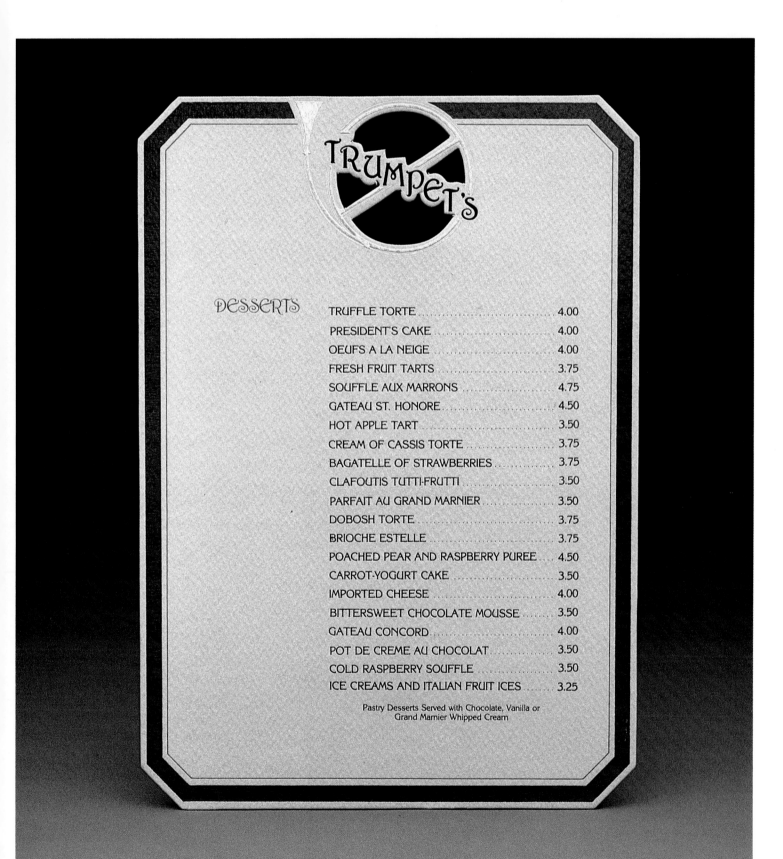

DESSERTS

TRUFFLE TORTE	4.00
PRESIDENT'S CAKE	4.00
OEUFS A LA NEIGE	4.00
FRESH FRUIT TARTS	3.75
SOUFFLE AUX MARRONS	4.75
GATEAU ST. HONORE	4.50
HOT APPLE TART	3.50
CREAM OF CASSIS TORTE	3.75
BAGATELLE OF STRAWBERRIES	3.75
CLAFOUTIS TUTTI-FRUTTI	3.50
PARFAIT AU GRAND MARNIER	3.50
DOBOSH TORTE	3.75
BRIOCHE ESTELLE	3.75
POACHED PEAR AND RASPBERRY PUREE	4.50
CARROT-YOGURT CAKE	3.50
IMPORTED CHEESE	4.00
BITTERSWEET CHOCOLATE MOUSSE	3.50
GATEAU CONCORD	4.00
POT DE CREME AU CHOCOLAT	3.50
COLD RASPBERRY SOUFFLE	3.50
ICE CREAMS AND ITALIAN FRUIT ICES	3.25

Pastry Desserts Served with Chocolate, Vanilla or
Grand Marnier Whipped Cream

Restaurant: T.G.I Friday's
Location: Nationwide chain headquartered in
Dallas, Texas
Designers: Luis Acevedo and Woody Pirtle
Firm: Pirtle Design
Illustrator: Luis Acevedo
Printer: Allcraft Printing
Specifications: T.G.I. Friday's Cappuccino Menu
Size: 3¾″ x 6⅛″

This espresso menu creates a humorous paradox and a
pun. What is that Capuchin monk, who denies all
earthly pleasures, doing inside such a sensuously
colored monastery? What will he do with that luscious
cappuccino in the pink cup, topped with mounds of
sinful whipped cream? Why, he'll drink it, of course.
Subtly, the menu art tells you that you won't be able to
resist the offerings of this menu either.

ESPRESSO Á LA EUROPA

ESPRESSO
A demitasse of the original.

ESPRESSO ROMANO
Espresso served in the Italian manner, with a twist of lemon.

ESPRESSO CON PANNA
Espresso topped with fresh whipped cream and shaved chocolate.

CAPPUCCINO
A traditional favorite: Espresso topped with thick foamed milk.

CAFFÈ LATTE
The Italian name. (Café Au Lait in France; Café Con Leche in Spain)
A lighter, milkier Cappuccino: foamed milk layered with espresso and topped with a sprinkling of nutmeg.

CAFFÈ CIOCCOLOCCINO (CHOCO LA CHEEN'O)
Espresso with chocolate ice cream, topped with foamed milk and shaved chocolate.

Any espresso drink may be ordered decaffeinated: The coffee will be brewed using a special freshly ground decaffeinated bean.

7

Children's Menus

Children don't ordinarily take home a paycheck, control
family finances, or make decisions such as where a family will
be eating dinner. As a result, they're often overlooked as a
major market by restaurants. But for years, supermarkets have
cleverly catered to children by placing brightly-colored cereal
and cookie boxes close to the floor, within the reach of
toddlers. What brilliant supermarket manager was it who first
placed candy racks next to the cash registers, right where
tired, impatient toddlers stand while waiting for mother or
father to get through a long checkout line?
A menu specifically designed to entertain and please a child
can be as valuable to the enjoyment of a family dinner as
having a babysitter at the table. Children's menus that
promote family participation can also help draw families
closer together. And like the brilliant marketing of
McDonald's, with its colorful giveaways and simple menus
custom designed for a child's palatte, a children's menu can
draw children into a restaurant.

Restaurant:	El Torito
Location:	Nationwide chain of Mexican restaurants
Designer:	Larry McAdams
Firm:	Larry McAdams Design, Inc.
Illustrator:	Larry McAdams
Printer:	Gardner/Fulmer
Specifications:	
Size:	8½″ x 11″ cover
Paper:	Kromecoat, one-sided

El Torito features a special children's menu which, on the inside, contains games and puzzles along with food listings. Designed as a take-home piece, the menu can be turned into a Spanish hacienda with stand-up paper dolls and a miniature taco. The hacienda is die-cut on durable Kromecoat stock. This menu has won awards and has been featured in several design publications.

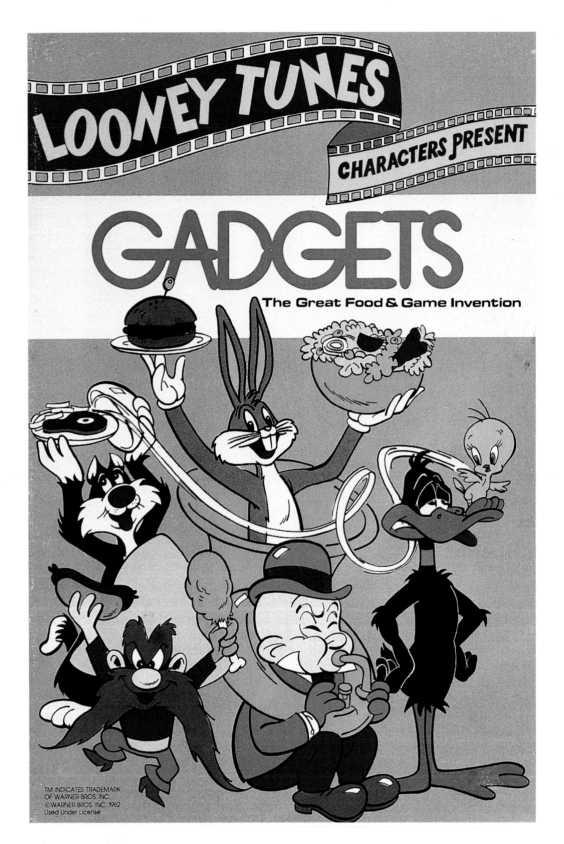

Restaurant: Gadgets
Location: East Rutherford, New Jersey
Designer: Lew Lehrman
Firm: Design Unlimited/Culinary Concepts
Illustrator: Looney Tunes™ Warner Brothers, Inc.
Printer: East Coast Lithographers
Specifications: Comic Book Menu
Size: 6¾″ x 10″
Paper: Coated stock

Gadgets is owned by Warner Leisure Corporation and uses Warner's licensed Looney Tunes™ characters as the theme for its menus. The comic book format is designed for all ages, but will especially appeal to children. Menu items are incorporated into brief cartoon stories, piquing the diner's interest in reading the entire comic book, as well as the menu.

Restaurant: Gadgets

Location: East Rutherford, New Jersey

Designer: Lew Lehrman

Firm: Design Unlimited/Culinary
Concepts

Illustrator: Looney Tunes™ Warner Brothers, Inc

Printer: East Coast Lithographers

Specifications: Porky Pig™ Menu

Size: 11″ x 8½″

Paper: Coated stock

The Porky Pig™ menu, designed for very young
children, appears with a pivoting arm which can
move to point to various riddles and reveal
answers. The riddles are on the front of the menu
and the menu selections are on the back.

CHILDREN'S MENU

CONNECT THE DOTS

For those under 12
(No matter how young you feel)

ALL ITEMS 99¢
INCLUDES BEVERAGE

WORD GAMES

See how many words you can find in the puzzle below. You will have to read forward, diagonally, or up and down. When you find a word draw a circle around it.

Help the waiter to unscramble the names of the different foods offered. (P.S. You can find the answers in the menu.)

```
E L T O R W T O P      PLANTS    NACHOS
F N W E T A C O L      WAITER    ENCHILADA
O A C A N T I N A      DISH      TILE
U C C H I P C I N      ONION     CARPET
N H A H I T E O T      TACO      TABLE
T O T A B L E N S      SALAD     CANTINA
A S D I S H A R T      TEA       CHIP
I L S A L A D D E      ICE       FOUNTAIN
N C A R P E T L A
```

1. rugbremha
2. octa
3. iruarbt
4. legdril shecee
5. toh ogd
6. antupe turbet
   nad yejil

Key
hamburger 4. grilled cheese
1. taco   5. hot dog
3. burrito   6. peanut butter and jelly

PEANUT BUTTER & JELLY

BURRITO

TACO

GRILLED CHEESE

HAMBURGER OR HOT DOG

INSTRUCTIONS FOR ASSEMBLING HOUSE

Step 1
Punch out house on perforated lines and fold on scored lines as shown. Also open door and windows.

Step 2
Lock in tabs on the edge of the house.

Step 3
Fold down flap "A" and tuck in flaps "B" and "C" inside "A".

Step 4
Tuck in flap "D" to complete assembly of the bottom of the house.

Step 5
Lock in tab of the roof between the bird and palm tree. Detach the children and the taco also. Bend tabs back so the children can stand up.

A

C

Restaurant: El Torito
Location: Nationwide chain of Mexican restaurants
Designer: Larry McAdams
Firm: Larry McAdams Design, Inc.
Illustrator: Larry McAdams
Printer: Gardner/Fulmer
Specifications:
Size: 8½" x 11" cover
Paper: Kromecoat, one-sided

El Torito features a special children's menu which, on the inside, contains games and puzzles along with food listings. Designed as a take-home piece, the menu can be turned into a Spanish hacienda with stand-up paper dolls and a miniature taco. The hacienda is die-cut on durable Kromecoat stock. This menu has won awards and has been featured in several design publications.

Restaurant: Crabapples
Location: Sturbridge, Massachusetts
Designer: Niki Bonnett
Firm: Niki Bonnett Design
Illustrator: Niki Bonnett
Printer: Multiprint
Specifications:
Size: 8½″ x 16″
Paper: Sunray Opaque Vellum
70# text off- white

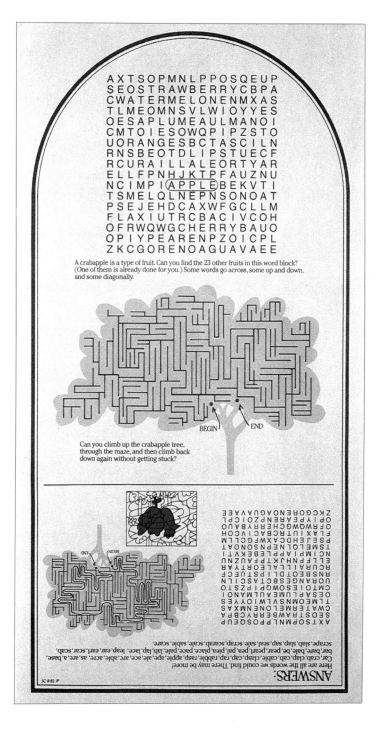

This inexpensively produced menu was designed as a take-home promotion piece to entertain children while they wait for their order to arrive. Printed on both sides with games and puzzles created by the designer, each having something to do with the Crabapple theme, the children's menu reinforces the design elements used in the adult menu. The regular Crabapples menu is featured in the Institutional chapter. The restaurant is part of the Restaurant Associates group.

Restaurant: Plata Grande Restaurant
Location: Beltsville, Maryland
Designers: Kathleen Wilmes Herring and
Michael David Brown
Firm: MDB Communications, Inc.
Illustrator: Kathleen Wilmes Herring
Printer: Peake Printers, Inc.
Specifications:
Size: 7¼″ x 10″ (outside edges of die-cut)
Paper: Kromecoat

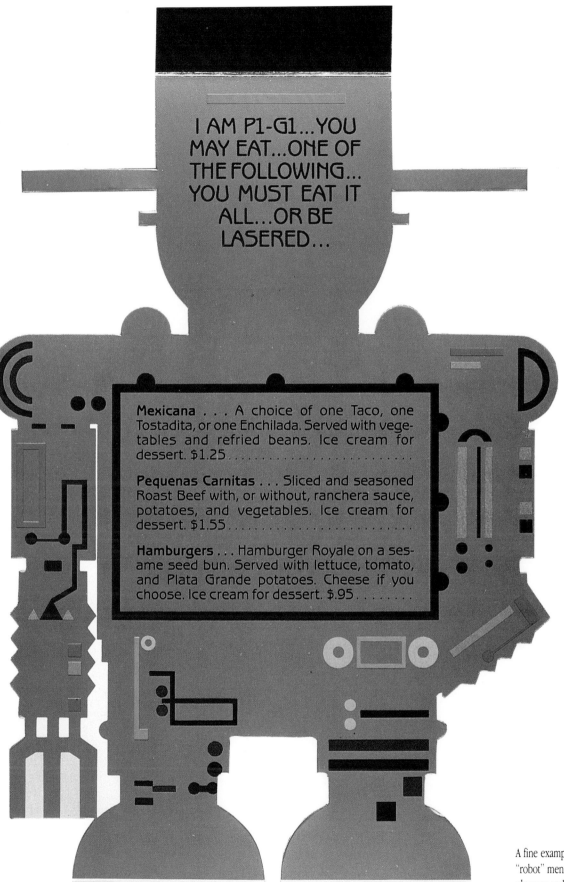

I AM P1-G1...YOU MAY EAT...ONE OF THE FOLLOWING... YOU MUST EAT IT ALL...OR BE LASERED...

Mexicana . . . A choice of one Taco, one Tostadita, or one Enchilada. Served with vegetables and refried beans. Ice cream for dessert. $1.25 . . . .

Pequenas Carnitas . . . Sliced and seasoned Roast Beef with, or without, ranchera sauce, potatoes, and vegetables. Ice cream for dessert. $1.55 . . . .

Hamburgers . . . Hamburger Royale on a sesame seed bun. Served with lettuce, tomato, and Plata Grande potatoes. Cheese if you choose. Ice cream for dessert. $.95 . . . .

A fine example of clever design, typeface, and copy, the "robot" menu was created entirely for children's pleasure and entertainment. It is also intended as a take-home promotional piece. The menu is printed in full color with silver metallic ink and a varnish top coating. The intricate die-cut robot character tells the children to "eat it all—or be lasered ...." The restaurant's main menu is in the Ethnic chapter.

Chocolate Coke
It's the real thing—with chocolate syrup.
$.95

Vanilla Coke
Coke with vanilla syrup.
$.95

Cherry Coke
Drugstore style with cherry syrup.
$.95

Chocolate Wizard
A creamy drink made with crumbled Oreo cookies and vanilla ice cream.
$1.50

Restaurant: T.G.I. Friday's
Location: Nationwide chain headquartered in Dallas, Texas
Designer: Ken Shafer
Firm: Pirtle Design
Illustrator: Ken Shafer
Printer: Allcraft Printing
Specifications: T.G.I. Friday's Kids' Drink Menu
Size: 6⅝″ x 12¾″
Paper: Kimdura

T.G.I. Friday's provides a menu for kids that features fun drinks, including three flavors of colas and a drink made of vanilla ice cream and Oreo cookies. Brightly colored silhouetted shapes of bottled drinks are printed on the cover. The inside copy is written with bold crayon in childish handwriting. The menu is printed on Kimdura, a durable synthetic paper—an excellent choice for children's menus.

Restaurant: Meyers'

Location: Quakertown, Pennsylvania

Designer: Robin Smith

Firm: Design Unlimited/
Culinary Concepts

Illustrator: Robin Smith

Printer: *Chicken Glasses:*
East Coast Lithographers
Moustaches: Artisan Printers

Specifications: Chicken Glasses and
Moustache Menus

Size: 15½″ x 10¼″

Paper: Hammermill Cover

Meyers' old-fashioned family restaurant provides two die-cut placemat menus for children 12 and under. One menu features moustaches which children can pop out and wear. The other menu contains hilarious pop-out-and-wear spectacles designed as two gossiping chickens whose wings suggest fluttering eyelashes. Both menus should entertain the entire family.

Meyers
Mustache Masquerade
For youngsters 12 and under

INSTRUCTIONS
Press out and carefully insert mustache into your nose.

Be a member of Meyers clean plate club
We'll put your name on our club roster, and give you a great big clean plate club button too!

Starters

Soup of the day	.75
Fresh fruit cocktail	.75
Chilled melon, in season	.75
Orange juice	.35

Favorite Samitches

Served with crispy potato chips and pickles. We'll trim away the crust if you like.

TUNA SALAD SANDWICH	1.25
GRILLED AMERICAN CHEESE	.85
WITH HAM OR BACON	1.10
WITH TOMATO	.95
B.L.T. Bacon, lettuce and tomato, of course!	1.00
SLICED WHITE MEAT TURKEY	1.25
PEANUT BUTTER 'N JELLY	.75
GRILLED HOT DOG	.80

DESIGN UNLIMITED, Hempstead, N.Y.

Kid Sized Meals

Served with potato and vegetable and milk or chocolate milk

GRILLED HAMBURGER STEAK	2.25
FRIED JUMBO SHRIMP (3)	4.25
BREADED OR BROILED FILLET OF SOLE	2.75
SLICED ROAST BEEF, BAKED HAM, OR ROAST TURKEY	2.50
BREADED FRIED CHICKEN (Drumstick and Thigh)	2.15
SOME SKETTIES Served with a small salad, choice of dressing	1.95

Selections are also available from our regular menu - at kids' prices, of course.

Junior Burgers

Served on a bun, with chips and pickle

HAMBURGER	.75
CHEESEBURGER	.85
BACON BURGER	.95
BACON CHEESEBURGER	1.05

Quarter pound hamburgers are also available

Quenchers

Milk	.40
Chocolate milk	.45
Coca Cola or Sprite	.45
Milkshake	.90
Orange or lime freeze	.90

Sweet Treats

Clown sundae	.75	Rice pudding	.75
	Ice cream	.60	
Small chocolate sundae	.75		

Order from our regular menu too!

MEYERS FAMILY RESTAURANT
501 N. West End Boulevard
Quakertown, Pennsylvania 18951   (215) 536-4422

8

Informal Dining

Informal restaurants include coffee shops, chain restaurants, pubs, and cafes. These restaurants cater to family dining, convenience dining, and singles as well. The interior decor is friendly and the customers could be local people who return repeatedly, or travelers just passing through.

The average price range is usually moderate, and checks can be large or small, depending upon one's budget, or what one chooses to spend. The entree selection ranges from inexpensive to expensive items, and it's possible to have a full meal or just a snack, dessert, or drink.

When restaurateurs stray from the look of the ordinary coffee shop menu, informal menus can be quite interesting. Some of these dining establishments have separate menus for breakfast, lunch, dinner, and drinks. Informal restaurants which cater largely to families may want to consider adding a separate children's menu for a friendly finishing touch.

Restaurant: Sneakers
Location: Miami, Florida
Designer: Milton Glaser
Firm: Milton Glaser, Inc.
Illustrator: Milton Glaser
Specifications:
Size: 7″ x 11″ cover
Paper: Kromecoat

Part of the complex of restaurants at The Towers of
Quayside, Sneakers accommodates the sporting crowd.
More casual than the formal dining rooms of the Great
House, Sneakers' main offerings are hors d'oeuvres.

Restaurant: Market Bar & Dining Room
Location: New York, New York
Designer: Milton Glaser
Firm: Milton Glaser, Inc.
Illustrator: Milton Glaser

Located in the World Trade Center, the Market Bar menu changes daily, depending upon the availability of foods and the quality offered by the various vendors in the wholesale food markets of the city. The most unusual feature of this menu is the listing of the wholesale vendor's name along with the food entry, so that any slip in the quality of produce, meats, or fish can be traced directly to the source—and no vendor wants to risk his or her good reputation. Also, customers appreciate the restaurant's concern with providing the best possible quality of food.

Market Bar

Dining Rooms

Fish & Shellfish Are Delivered Fresh Each Day

We sell our coffee, all Colombian, in one-pound bags. Ask the headwaiter.

Our Specialties:
Shell-roasted clams
Butcher cuts, charcoal broiled
Fulton Market seafood stew
Vegetables steamed to order
Apple Strudel

APPETIZERS COLD	Clams, little necks or topnecks	4.25
	Oysters: we only serve Cotuits	4.50
Shellfish dressings: pepper-vinaigrette, dill mayonnaise or spicy red sauce	Chilled shrimp w. fresh horseradish	5.50
	Raw sliced beef, parmesan dressing	3.95
	Chef's terrine	(daily price)
	Spinach & watercress salad w. feta cheese	3.50
HOT	Wild mushrooms in pastry shell	3.95
	Shrimp & crabmeat fritters w. devil sauce	5.50
	Little neck clams, baked or shell-roasted	4.50
	Baked oysters, stuffed w. mushrooms & shrimp	4.50
SOUPS & CHOWDERS	French Market onion soup, baked w. cheese	3.95
	This day's soup	2.25
BUTCHER CUTS	**Roast Prime Rib of Beef**	14.75
	12 oz. Rump Steak, luncheon cut, w. roasted peppers	13.95
Grilled over charcoal	**Sirloin Steak,** New York cut	17.75
	10 oz. Tenderloin of Beef	14.75
	Grilled Veal Chop	13.50
Butcher cuts come with crisped onions	**Charred Ground Round**	8.50
	Calf's Liver Steak, grilled or sauteed	10.50
	Double Breast of Chicken, marinated in lemon & sage	9.75
	Brochette of Marinated Lamb	10.50
	Fillets in a Skillet, smothered mushrooms & bordelaise sauce	13.50
CLAM HOUSE COOKING	**Fulton Market Seafood Stew**	13.25
	Large Shrimp, deep fried in beer batter w. pepperslaw or panfried with tomatoes & peppers	11.50
	Poached Filet of Red Snapper w. fresh vegetables	12.95
	Bay Scallops in Creole or Chablis Sauce	11.50
	Mussels Steamed in White Wine fresh cream & herbs	7.50
	Broiled Swordfish w. lemon butter	13.50
	Filet of Sole, panfried or broiled	11.25

MARKET SPECIALS

Prepared from seasonal plentifuls that are supplied by established first-class purveyors in the city's wholesale markets.

JOS. KENNEY & CO.
Purveyors of fine meats & meat products
Melon with prosciutto ham *3.50*

GAETANO CALARCO & CO.
Wholesale Foreign & Domestic Fruit
Smoked Westphalian Ham w. fresh horseradish *4.25*

DeBRAGGA and SPITLER
Meats, poultry, provisions
Endive Salad with walnut dressing *2.50*

HYGRADE FISH PRODUCTS
Fresh & Portioned
Broiled fresh Codfish with lemon butter *9.25*

PACIFIC SEH
Prime Meats & Poultry
Panfried Chicken Breast with stringbeans *10.50*

GEORGE M. STILL, INC.
Finest of Clams & Oysters since 1857
Breaded filet of Sole with todays vegetable *10.95*

LONG ISLAND BEEF CO.
Fine Prime Beef
Stuffed Breast of Veal with mushroom risotto *11.25*

DROHAN CO. INC.
Food specialists, poultry, game
Frittata with chorizo and tomato *7.25*

M.H. GREENEBAUM INC.
Importers, exporters, purveyors, packers
Pear tart *2.95*

B. EISNER
Fresh fruit & produce
Fresh Strawberries *2.95*

DOMS MARKET
Purveyors of Fine Fruit & Produce
Cream of Carrot Soup *2.25*

WATERMAN-LEDER CORP.
Fruits & Vegetables
Braised Fennel w. cheese glaze *2.25*

Carafe of Red or White Wine *9.00*

Ask for our special wine sold by the glass *3.00*

We are not responsible for articles lost or exchanged on the premises, nor for deals and bargains struck during meal periods.

Frittata of the Day	7.25	**EGGS & HASHES**
Corned Beef Hash w. fried egg	7.50	
Fried in their skins	2.25	**POTATOES**
Home fried or French fried	2.25	
Broccoli w. hollandaise sauce	2.75	**FRESH VEGETABLES & SALADS**
This day's vegetable	(market price)	
Onion crisps	2.25	
Platter of Market Vegetables, green herb butter	7.50	
Beefsteak tomato & onion slices w. cracked pepper & basil dressing	2.95	
Mixed Green Salad	2.25	Roquefort-cognac dressing add 1.00
Chef's Market Salad w. meats, cheese & avocado	8.95	**COLD DISHES**
Tartar Steak, ground to order	9.25	
Crabmeat, Shrimp & Avocado Salad	12.95	
Bowl of fresh cut fruits	2.50	**DESSERTS**
Hot fresh pineapple, vanilla ice cream	3.75	
Baked Cheesecake	2.75	
Chocolate Cake	2.75	Our cakes & pastries are baked here every day.
Marinated berries w. vanilla ice cream	2.95	
Frozen Chocolate Souffle, burnt almond sauce	2.95	
Bassett's vanilla ice cream w. maple syrup	3.25	
Fresh Tart of the Day	2.95	
Homemade apple strudel w. vanilla sauce	3.25	
Pot of Tea Leaves:		**BEVERAGES**
Earl Grey's or Darjeeling	1.50	We pour heavy cream with our coffee.
Coffee	1.50	
Espresso	1.75	
Cappuccino	2.25	

Reservations accepted for evening parties and special events.

Our Matches & Ash Trays Are Put Up In Sets For Sale

Restaurant: Blue Ribbon Delicatessen & Cafe
Location: Kansas City, Missouri
Designer: Milton Glaser
Firm: Milton Glaser, Inc.
Illustrator: Milton Glaser
Printer: Creative Printing Company, Inc.
Specifications:
Size: 8″ x 10″ cover
Paper: 80# Velcoat Matte Cover

The menu cover has a clean, fresh design and opens to a comment regarding the freshness of the food. The menu pages are separated into tabbed sections. A humorous element of this menu is the small man at the bottom of each page who gets fatter and fatter as the menu progresses.

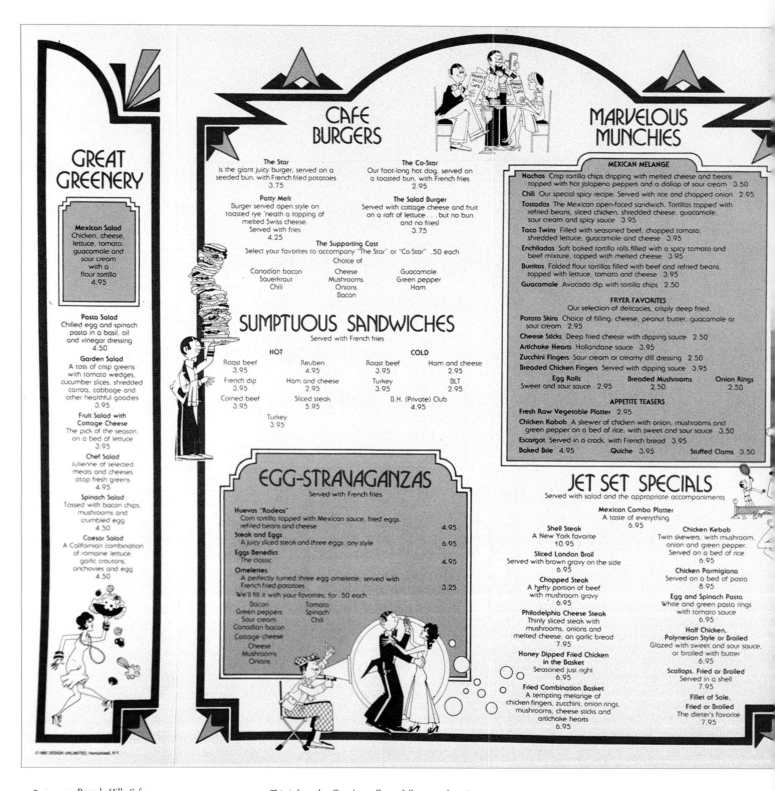

GREAT GREENERY

Mexican Salad
Chicken, cheese, lettuce, tomato, guacamole and sour cream with a flour tortilla
4.95

Pasta Salad
Chilled egg and spinach pasta in a basil, oil and vinegar dressing
4.50

Garden Salad
A toss of crisp greens with tomato wedges, cucumber slices, shredded carrots, cabbage and other healthful goodies
3.95

Fruit Salad with Cottage Cheese
The pick of the season, on a bed of lettuce
3.95

Chef Salad
Julienne of selected meats and cheeses atop fresh greens
4.95

Spinach Salad
Tossed with bacon chips, mushrooms and crumbled egg
4.50

Caesar Salad
A Californian combination of romaine lettuce, garlic croutons, anchovies and egg
4.50

CAFE BURGERS

The Star
is the giant juicy burger, served on a seeded bun, with French fried potatoes
3.75

Patty Melt
Burger served open style on toasted rye 'neath a topping of melted Swiss cheese. Served with fries
4.25

The Co-Star
Our foot-long hot dog, served on a toasted bun, with French fries
2.95

The Salad Burger
Served with cottage cheese and fruit on a raft of lettuce . . . but no bun and no fries!
3.75

The Supporting Cast
Select your favorites to accompany "The Star" or "Co-Star" .50 each
Choice of

Canadian bacon	Cheese	Guacamole
Sauerkraut	Mushrooms	Green pepper
Chili	Onions	Ham
	Bacon	

SUMPTUOUS SANDWICHES
Served with French fries

HOT

Roast beef 3.95	Reuben 4.95
French dip 3.95	Ham and cheese 2.95
Corned beef 3.95	Sliced steak 5.95
	Turkey 3.95

COLD

Roast beef 3.95	Ham and cheese 2.95
Turkey 3.95	BLT 2.95
B.H. (Private) Club 4.95	

EGG-STRAVAGANZAS
Served with French fries

Huevos "Rodeos"
Corn tortilla topped with Mexican sauce, fried eggs, refried beans and cheese — 4.95

Steak and Eggs
A juicy sliced steak and three eggs, any style — 6.95

Eggs Benedict
The classic — 4.95

Omelettes
A perfectly turned three egg omelette, served with French fried potatoes — 3.25
We'll fill it with your favorites, for .50 each

Bacon	Tomato
Green peppers	Spinach
Sour cream	Chili
Canadian bacon	
Cottage cheese	
Cheese	
Mushrooms	
Onions	

MARVELOUS MUNCHIES

MEXICAN MELANGE

Nachos Crisp tortilla chips dripping with melted cheese and beans topped with hot jalapeno peppers and a dollop of sour cream 3.50

Chili Our special spicy recipe. Served with rice and chopped onion 2.95

Tostadas The Mexican open-faced sandwich. Tortillas topped with refried beans, sliced chicken, shredded cheese, guacamole, sour cream and spicy sauce 3.95

Taco Twins Filled with seasoned beef, chopped tomato, shredded lettuce, guacamole and cheese 3.95

Enchiladas Soft baked tortilla rolls filled with a spicy tomato and beef mixture, topped with melted cheese 3.95

Burritos Folded flour tortillas filled with beef and refried beans, topped with lettuce, tomato and cheese 3.95

Guacamole Avocado dip with tortilla chips 2.50

FRYER FAVORITES
Our selection of delicacies, crisply deep fried.

Potato Skins Choice of filling: cheese, peanut butter, guacamole or sour cream 2.95

Cheese Sticks Deep fried cheese with dipping sauce 2.50

Artichoke Hearts Hollandaise sauce 3.95

Zucchini Fingers Sour cream or creamy dill dressing 2.50

Breaded Chicken Fingers Served with dipping sauce 3.95

Egg Rolls Sweet and sour sauce 2.95	**Breaded Mushrooms** 2.50	**Onion Rings** 2.50

APPETITE TEASERS

Fresh Raw Vegetable Platter 2.95

Chicken Kabob A skewer of chicken with onion, mushrooms and green pepper on a bed of rice, with sweet and sour sauce 3.50

Escargot Served in a crock, with French bread 3.95

Baked Brie 4.95	**Quiche** 3.95	**Stuffed Clams** 3.50

JET SET SPECIALS
Served with salad and the appropriate accompaniments

Mexican Combo Platter
A taste of everything
6.95

Shell Steak
A New York favorite
10.95

Sliced London Broil
Served with brown gravy on the side
6.95

Chopped Steak
A hefty portion of beef with mushroom gravy
6.95

Philadelphia Cheese Steak
Thinly sliced steak with mushrooms, onions and melted cheese, on garlic bread
7.95

Honey Dipped Fried Chicken in the Basket
Seasoned just right
6.95

Fried Combination Basket
A tempting melange of chicken fingers, zucchini, onion rings, mushrooms, cheese sticks and artichoke hearts
6.95

Chicken Kebab
Twin skewers, with mushroom, onion and green pepper. Served on a bed of rice
6.95

Chicken Parmigiana
Served on a bed of pasta
8.95

Egg and Spinach Pasta
White and green pasta rings with tomato sauce
6.95

**Half Chicken,
Polynesian Style or Broiled**
Glazed with sweet and sour sauce, or broiled with butter
6.95

Scallops, Fried or Broiled
Served in a shell
7.95

**Fillet of Sole,
Fried or Broiled**
The dieter's favorite
7.95

© 1982 DESIGN UNLIMITED, Hempstead, N.Y.

Restaurant:	Beverly Hills Cafe
Location:	Long Island, New York
Designer:	Lew Lehrman
Firm:	Design Unlimited/Culinary Concepts
Illustrator:	Bill Kresse
Printer:	East Coast Lithographers
Specifications:	
Size:	7″ x 16″ cover
Paper:	Curtis Linen Cover

This informal coffee shop offers a full range of entries and serves regular meals as well as after-movie snacks. The menu's cartoon-like illustrations and humorous copy set the tone for a casual and relaxing atmosphere, evocative of the 1920s.

SOUPS

Pizza Soup
Spiced tomato crusted
in the crock with
melted cheese
2.95

Pea Soup
With ham and cheese
2.50

French Onion au Gratin
Baked in the crock
with a crust of
melted cheese
2.95

BEVERAGES

Espresso 1.25	Tea .75
Cappuccino 1.75	Mineral Water 1.50
Coffee .75	Soft Drinks 1.00
Sanka .75	Juices 1.25
	Milk .75

BEER
On Tap

Michelob Lite 1.75	Budweiser 1.75
	Beck's 2.00

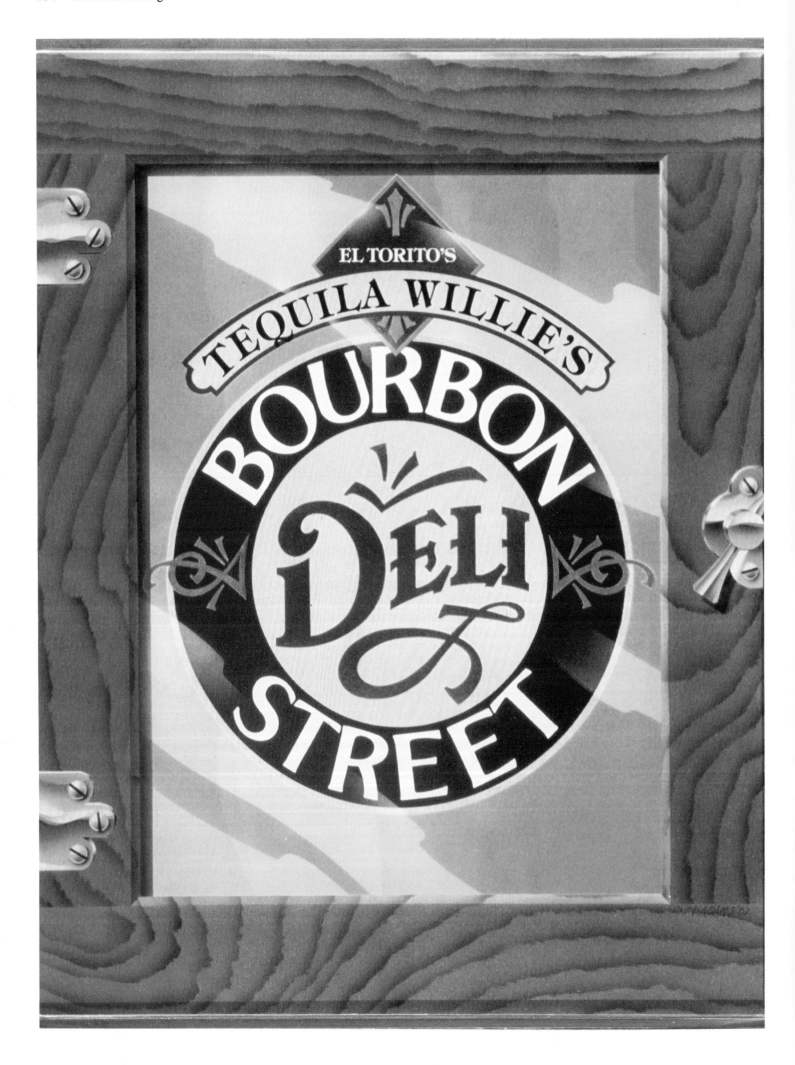

Restaurant: Tequila Willie's
Location: Nationwide chain owned by El Torito, headquartered in Irvine, California
Designer: Larry McAdams
Firm: Larry McAdams Design, Inc.
Illustrator: Larry McAdams
Calligrapher: Larry McAdams
Specifications:
Size: 8″ x 10″ cover

This restaurant belongs to a nationwide chain which offers an array of fresh foods. Cover artwork consists of full-color paintings, suggestive of New Orleans. Clients of this restaurant are mostly young professionals and families.

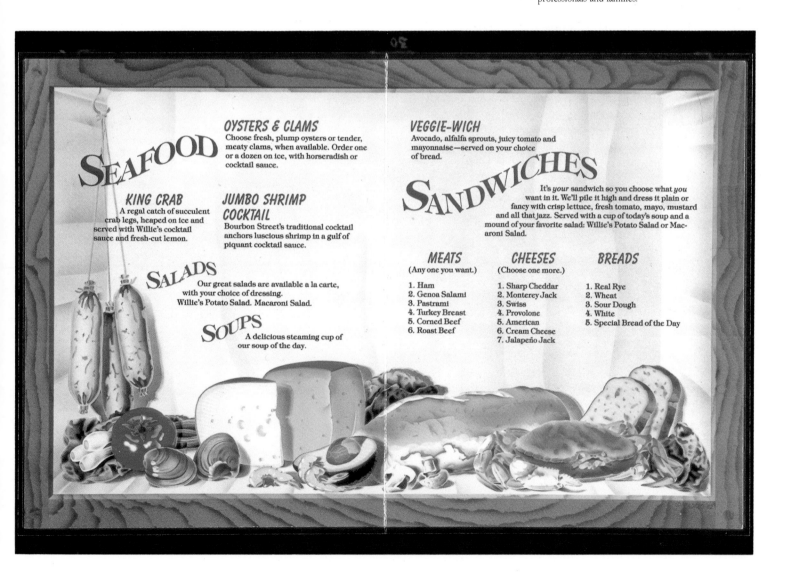

SEAFOOD

KING CRAB
A regal catch of succulent crab legs, heaped on ice and served with Willie's cocktail sauce and fresh-cut lemon.

OYSTERS & CLAMS
Choose fresh, plump oysters or tender, meaty clams, when available. Order one or a dozen on ice, with horseradish or cocktail sauce.

JUMBO SHRIMP COCKTAIL
Bourbon Street's traditional cocktail anchors luscious shrimp in a gulf of piquant cocktail sauce.

SALADS

Our great salads are available a la carte, with your choice of dressing. Willie's Potato Salad. Macaroni Salad.

SOUPS

A delicious steaming cup of our soup of the day.

VEGGIE-WICH

Avocado, alfalfa sprouts, juicy tomato and mayonnaise—served on your choice of bread.

SANDWICHES

It's *your* sandwich so you choose what *you* want in it. We'll pile it high and dress it plain or fancy with crisp lettuce, fresh tomato, mayo, mustard and all that jazz. Served with a cup of today's soup and a mound of your favorite salad: Willie's Potato Salad or Macaroni Salad.

MEATS (Any one you want.)	CHEESES (Choose one more.)	BREADS
1. Ham	1. Sharp Cheddar	1. Real Rye
2. Genoa Salami	2. Monterey Jack	2. Wheat
3. Pastrami	3. Swiss	3. Sour Dough
4. Turkey Breast	4. Provolone	4. White
5. Corned Beef	5. American	5. Special Bread of the Day
6. Roast Beef	6. Cream Cheese	
	7. Jalapeño Jack	

Restaurant: Swiss Chalet
Location: Nationwide food chain
Designer: Ambrose Carr Linton & DeForest
Printer: Graphics for Production
Specifications:
    Size: 9½" x 13"

The Swiss Chalet is a family-style restaurant serving
chicken and ribs. Its menu is fully illustrated with
pictures of fresh ingredients against a farm
background.

STATE RESTAURANT ASSOCIATIONS

Alaska Cabaret, Hotel and Restaurant Association
P.O. Box 4-1260
Anchorage, AK 99509
Att: Robert R. Cramer
(907) 272-8133

Alabama Restaurant and Food Service Association
2100 Data Drive, Suite 207
Birmingham, AL 35224
Att: Stewart McLaurin
(206) 988-9880

Arizona Restaurant Association
112 North Central, Suite 417
Phoenix, AZ 85004
Att: Joe Banks
(602) 258-3256

Southern Arizona Restaurant Association
Tucson Chamber of Commerce Building
465 West St. Mary's Road., Suite 300
Tucson, AZ 85705
Att: Penelope Miedaner
(602) 791-9106

Arkansas Hospitality Association
603 Pulaski Street
P.O. Box 1556
Little Rock, AR 72203
Att: Maurice Lewis
(501) 376-2323

California Restaurant Association
3780 Wilshire Boulevard,
Suite 600
Los Angeles, CA 90010
Att: Stanley Kyker
(213) 384-1200

California State Restaurant Association
1225 8th Street, Suite 325
Sacramento, CA 95814
Att: Timothy Flanigan
(916) 447-5793

California Restaurant Association
355 Grand Avenue
Oakland, CA 94610
Att: Lea Adza
(415) 836-2588

Golden Gate Restaurant Association
291 Geary Street, Suite 515
San Francisco, CA 94102
Att: Guy Leonard
(415) 781-5348

Colorado-Wyoming Restaurant Association
1365 Logan Street
Denver, CO 80203
Att: Donald Quinn
(303) 830-2972

Connecticut Restaurant Association
236 Hamilton
Hartford, CT 06106
Att: Gary Hotchkin
(203) 247-7797

Delaware Restaurant Association
P.O. Box 7838
Newark, DE 19711
Att: Irene Beardwood
(302) 366-8565

Restaurant Association of Metropolitan Washington, Inc.
South Tysons Office Park
2112-D Gallows Road
Vienna, VA 22180
Att: John S. Cockrell
(703) 356-1315

Florida Restaurant Association
1065 NE 125th Street, Suite 409
North Miami, FL 33161
Att: Lois Kostroski
(305) 891-1852

Georgia Hospitality and Travel Association
148 International Boulevard
Suite 625
Atlanta, GA 30303
Att: Bob King
(404) 577-5888

Courtesy of the National Restaurant Association

Hawaii Restaurant Association
130 Merchant Street, #2020
Honolulu, HI 96813
Att: Helen Ettinger
(808) 536-9105

Kansas Restaurant Association
359 South Hydraulic
Wichita, KS 67211
Att: Bill Morris
(316) 267-8383

Michigan Restaurant Association
Executive Building, Suite 205
690 East Maple
Birmingham, MI 48011
Att: Ruth Ellen Mayhall
(313) 645-9770

Idaho Restaurant and Beverage Association
P.O. Box 8205
Boise, ID 83707
Att: William Roden
(208) 336-7930

Kentucky Restaurant Association
455 River City Mall
Suite 417-421 Starks Building
Louisville, KY 40202
Att: Joan Kemper
(502) 587-8629

Minnesota Restaurant and Foodservice Association
2001 University Avenue
St. Paul, MN 55104
Att: Arnold Hewes
(612) 647-0107

Illinois Restaurant Association
20 North Wacker Drive, Suite 1130
Chicago, IL 60606
Att: Andrew Kelly
(313) 372-6200

Louisiana Restaurant Association
3350 Ridgelake Drive, Suite 101
Metairie, LA 70002
Att: Jim Funk
(504) 831-7788

Mississippi Restaurant Association
P.O. Box 16395
Jackson, MS 39206
Att: Judy Shute
(601) 982-4281

Indiana Restaurant Association
2120 North Meridian Street
Indianapolis, IN 46202
Att: Warren Spangle
(317) 924-5106

Maine Restaurant Association
124 Sewall Street
Augusta, ME 04330
Att: Carl Sanford
(207) 623-2178

Missouri Restaurant Association
P.O. Box 10210
Kansas City, MO 64111
Att: Carl Degen
(816) 753-5222

Iowa Restaurant Association
415 Shops Building
Des Moines, IA 50309
Att: Les Davis
(515) 282-8304

Massachusetts Restaurant Association
825 Washington Street
Newtonville, MA 02160
Att: Raymond Murgia
(617) 969-3140

Missouri Restaurant Association
St. Louis Area
2385 Hampton Avenue, Suite 111
St. Louis, MO 63139
Att: Bill Ward

Montana Restaurant Association
P.O. Box 908
Helena, MT 59624
Att: Don Pratt
(406) 442-1432

Nebraska Restaurant Association
1220 Lincoln Benefit Building
Lincoln, NB 68508
Att: Herman Siefkes
(402) 475-4647

Nevada Restaurant Association
3661 Maryland Parkway, Suite 108
Las Vegas, NV 89109
Att: Van Heffner
(702) 733-1962

New Hampshire Hospitality Association
172 North Maine
Concord, NH 03301
Att: Executive Vice President
(603) 228-9585

New Mexico Restaurant Association
2130 San Mateo Boulevard NE
Suite C
Albuquerque, NM 87110
Att: Jack Ruggs
(505) 268-2474

New York State Restaurant Association
250 West 57th Street
New York, NY 10019
Att: Fred Sampson
(212) 246-3434

New York State Restaurant Association
3686 Gardenia Drive
Baldwinsville, NY 13027
Att: Rick Sampson
(315) 652-6555

North Carolina Restaurant Association
P.O. Box 6528
Raleigh, NC 27628
Att: T. Jerry Williams
(919) 782-5022

North Dakota Hospitality Association
P.O. Box 428
Bismark, ND 58501
Att: Executive Secretary
(701) 223-3313

Northeastern Ohio Restaurant Association
129 Main Street #1
Chardon, OH 44024
Att: Roberta Halford
(216) 621-7914

Northwestern Ohio Restaurant Association
1955 South Reynolds Road, Suite 16
Toledo, OH 42614
Att: Cheryl Drew
(419) 389-0501

Ohio State Restaurant Association
1061 Country Club Road
Columbus, OH 43227
Att: Tim Pond
(614) 864-2800

Oklahoma Restaurant Association
3800 North Portland
Oklahoma City, OK 73103
Att: Justin Hill
(405) 334-3180

Restaurant Association of Maryland, Inc.
5602 Baltimore National Pike
Suburbia Building, Suite 305
Baltimore, MD 21228
Att: Letitia Carter
(301) 788-6400

Restaurants of Oregon Association
3724 North east Broadway
Portland, OR 97232
Att: Helen Cover
(503) 249-0974

Pennsylvania Association of Travel and
Hospitality
5403 Carlisle Pike
Mechanicsburg, PA 17055
Att: Ronni Hannaman
(717) 697-3646

South Carolina Restaurant Association
510 Barringer Building
1338 Main Street
Columbia, SC 29201
Att: John Riddick
(803) 254-3906

Vermont Hotel-Motel and Restaurant
Association
P.O. Box 9
Montpelier, VT 05602
Att: Michael Yaroschuck
(802) 229-0062

Pennsylvania Restaurant Association
900 Eisenhower Boulevard, Suite C
Harrisburg, PA 17111
Att: Executive Vice President
(717) 939-7881

South Dakota Restaurant Assoc
805 ½ South Main Avenue
Sioux Falls, SD 57104
Att: Florence Holten
(605) 338-4906

Virginia Restaurant Association
2101 Libbie Avenue
Richmond, VA 23230
Att: Herbert Clegg
(804) 288-3065

Philadelphia-Delaware Valley Restaurant
Association
1131 L.V.B. Building
1700 Market Street
Philadelphia, PA 19103
Att: Mary Grant
(215) 567-6528

Tennessee Restaurant Association
229 Court Square
Franklin, TN 37064
Att: Ron Hart
(615) 790-2703

Restaurant Association of the State of
Washington, Inc.
722 Securities Guilding
Seattle, WA 98101
Att: John Gordon
(206) 682-6174

Texas Restaurant Association
P.O. Box 1429
Austin, TX 78767
Att: W.H. "Buckshot" Price
(512) 444-6543

Western Pennsylvania Restaurant and
Hospitality Association
1422 Bigelow Apartments
Pittsburgh, PA 15219
Att: Burt Young
(412) 288-0157

West Virginia Restaurant & Licensed
Beverage Association
P.O. Box 2391
Charlestown, WV 25328
Att: Thomas Tinder
(304) 342-6511

Utah Restaurant Association
2520 South State, Suite 221
Salt Lake City, UT 84-15
Att: Ronald Morgan
(801) 487-4821

Rhode Island Hospitality Association
P.O. Box 415
Ashton, RI 02869
Att: David Balfour
(401) 334-3180

Wisconsin Restaurant Association
122 West-Washington Avenue
Madison, WS 53703
Att: Ed Lump
(608) 251-3663